BLUE PLANET

Written by Barbara Embury Hehner

in consultation with Ted A. Maxwell, Ph.D.
Chairman, Center for Earth and Planetary Studies
National Air and Space Museum
Smithsonian Institution

WIDE WORLD SERIES

Gulliver Books

Harcourt Brace Jovanovich, Publishers

San Diego   New York   London

This book is based on the film **Blue Planet**, *funded by the Lockheed Corporation and the Smithsonian Institution's National Air and Space Museum, in cooperation with the National Aeronautics and Space Administration (NASA).*

First U.S. Edition

Library of Congress Cataloging-in-Publication Data
Hehner, Barbara.
        Blue planet / by Barbara Embury Hehner.
            p.   cm.
"Gulliver Books."
Summary: Explores, in text and photographs, the various ecosystems of the Earth
and how humans are affecting the delicate balance of the natural world.
ISBN 0-15-200423-8
1. Earth—Juvenile literature. 2. Geophysics—Juvenile
literature. [1. Earth. 2. Geophysics.] I. Title.
QC631.2.H44 1992
508—dc20 91-44094

With special thanks for the cooperation of the Book Development Division of the Smithsonian Institution Press

IMAX® is a registered trademark of Imax Corporation, 38 Isabella Street, Toronto, Ontario, M4Y 1N1.

Produced by Somerville House Books Ltd., 3080 Yonge Street, Suite 5000, Toronto, Ontario, Canada M4N 3N1.
Printed in Singapore
Designed by Andrew Smith and Annabelle Stanley / Andrew Smith Graphics Inc.
Illustrations by David Chapman
Indexing by Heather L. Ebbs
Smithsonian picture research by Paula Ballo-Dailey
Special thanks to Steven Soter, National Air and Space Museum

ABCDE

The author wishes to dedicate this book in memory of Eric O. W. Hehner, 1912-1990.

Many people contributed to the production of this book, but the author would particularly like to thank the following people for combining a high level of professional expertise with empathy and a sense of humor: Patrick Crean, Editorial Director, Somerville House Books; Caroline Newman and Paula Dailey, respectively Executive Editor for Book Development and Picture Editor at the Smithsonian Institution Press; and Ted A. Maxwell, Chairman, Center for Earth and Planetary Studies, National Air and Space Museum, Smithsonian Institution.

Title page photograph: *The Hubbard Glacier in Alaska, "calving" icebergs.*
Glaciers are just small remnants of the great ice sheets that retreated some 10,000 years ago.

Opposite page: *A Landsat satellite view of the Hubbard Glacier in Alaska. Over the last million years,*
great sheets of ice have advanced and retreated several times, covering northern Europe and much of North America.

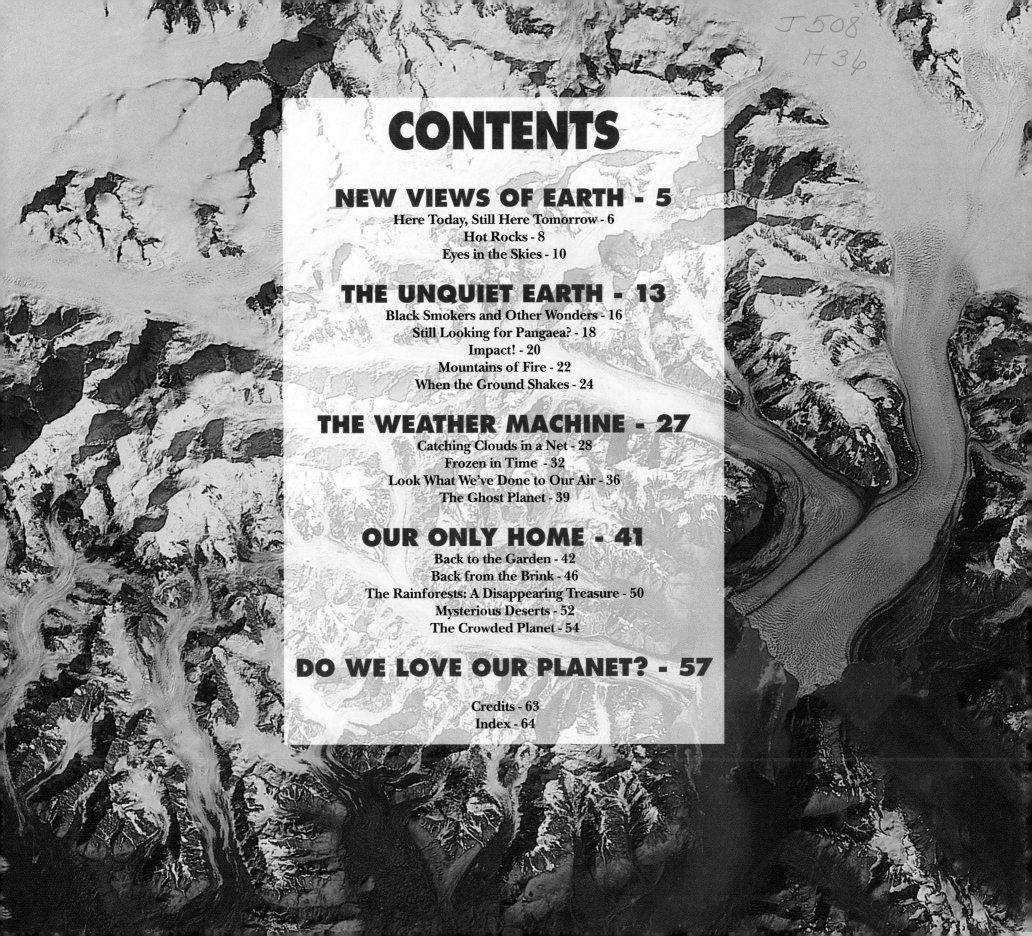

CONTENTS

NEW VIEWS OF EARTH - 5

THE UNQUIET EARTH - 13

THE WEATHER MACHINE - 27

OUR ONLY HOME - 41

DO WE LOVE OUR PLANET? - 57

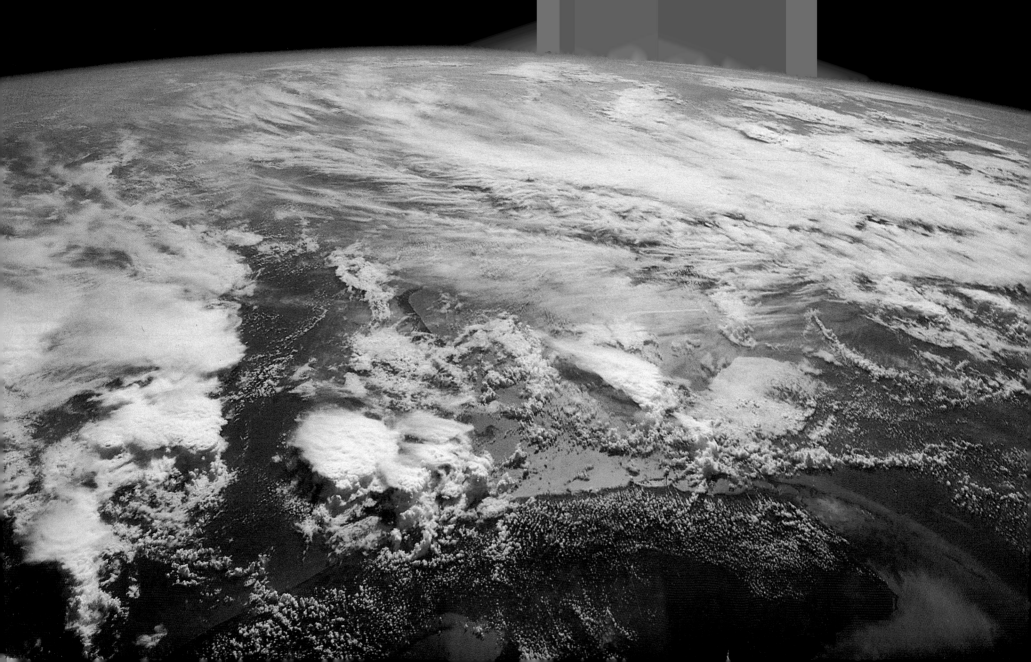

NEW VIEWS OF EARTH

Only about 300 men and women have ever gone into space. But the images of Earth they shared with the rest of us have forever changed how we see our planet. More than 20 years ago, Apollo astronauts photographed Earth from its closest neighbor, the Moon. From almost a quarter of a million miles away, our home planet looks like a glittering blue-and-white jewel in the blackness of space. Earth reflects the Sun's light far more brightly than the Moon does, shining like a beacon for lonely space voyagers.

Michael Collins, like many of the astronauts who visited the barren, airless, and waterless Moon, was filled with protective feelings for Earth. He compared our planet to a "delicate Christmas tree ornament." "I wish I had some way of protecting it, of keeping it pristine," he wrote. "It looks so clean and yet it is so dirty, in places at least. The boundary line between a blue-and-white planet, and one that is gray and tan, is fragile."

Today's shuttle astronauts are usually in orbit only 250 miles (400 kilometers) from Earth's surface. From that distance, a detailed and ever-changing panorama is on display. They can see that two-thirds of Earth's surface is water. Varying shades of blue and turquoise mark the places where oceans, seas, and rivers meet and mingle. Clouds move over sea and land in restless swirling patterns. The astronauts can see lightning flashes traveling hundreds of miles from cloud top to cloud top. They can see the sinister beauty of a hurricane, spreading its spiraling pinwheel arms over the Caribbean.

These are the outward signs of the great natural cycles that power Earth and make all life possible. Earth and its atmosphere form a closed system, and everything in the system is recycled — air, water, and even solid rock. Everything on Earth is in motion and everything is interconnected. Changes in one place will always cause changes somewhere else. We have learned that when rains are heavy in West Africa, Atlantic hurricanes are more devastating. And a powerful volcanic eruption — whether it's El Chichón in Mexico or Mount Pinatubo in the Philippines — may make temperatures cooler everywhere in the world for several years.

Our planet has great powers of healing and cleansing, but there are limits to these powers. From the shuttle, the astronauts can clearly see how fragile Earth is and how heedlessly human beings have damaged

Above: Europe, Asia, and parts of Africa can be seen in this photograph taken from the Apollo 11 *spacecraft approximately 100,000 miles (160,000 kilometers) from Earth.*

Left: Howard Russell Butler's oil painting "The Earth as Seen from the Moon" imagines a view that the Apollo astronauts would first see with their own eyes more than 30 years later.

Opposite page: From space, Earth is revealed as a watery planet, with land — in this view, Florida — rising here and there from its deep blue surface.

HERE TODAY, STILL HERE TOMORROW

Dulcie Atoll is one of the most remote places on Earth. This small, uninhabited island in the Pacific Ocean is 3,000 miles (4,800 kilometers) from the nearest continent. Yet a scientist who recently visited this island found 953 pieces of human-produced garbage washed up on the beach. These included 171 bottles, 25 shoes, seven aerosol cans, three cigarette lighters, and half a toy airplane. Most of these things — made of glass, plastic, and metal — will still

Huge landfill sites like this one are scattered all over North America, reminding us that there is no such thing as "getting rid of our garbage."

be there hundreds of years from now, unless we make an effort to clean them up. Glass bottles take about 100 years to break down; aluminum cans take 300 to 500 years to decay; and the plastic rings used to hold cans together last for about 450 years. By then, Dulcie Atoll could be piled high with thousands upon thousands of such things. But its problems are nothing in comparison with the beaches of the United States. During the 1990 National Beach Cleanup, volunteers collected 4,227,791 pieces of garbage in just three weeks, including over 100,000 plastic bottles, over 150,000 glass bottles, and over 150,000 aluminum cans!

What if the junk that chokes Dulcie Atoll (and beaches everywhere else in the world) were recycled instead? Glass bottles can be reused. Or they can be crushed into cullet, which is then mixed with sand, limestone, and soda ash and heated in a furnace to make new glass. Aluminum cans can be shredded, melted, and pressed into sheets of pure aluminum.

Reusing and recycling does more than keep our beaches clean: it also saves energy. Melting down and reusing an aluminum can, for example, uses only ten percent of the energy needed to make the original can. Yet in 1990, North Americans threw away enough aluminum to build all the airplanes of all the North American airlines. In that year, North Americans recycled only about ten percent of their trash, while Japan recycled 50 percent. Remote, polluted Dulcie Atoll reminds us of what one environmentalist, Barry Commoner, said: "Everything in the system stays in the system. There is no 'away'."

it. The world's great rivers — from the United States's Mississippi and South America's Orinoco and Amazon to China's Yangtze and Madagascar's Betsiboka — spew greater and greater loads of eroded topsoil and chemical pollutants into the oceans. Ugly brown stains, visible from space, now mark the mouths of these rivers. The astronauts can also see smoke rising high into the atmosphere over South America, where one of Earth's great treasures, the Amazon rainforest, is burning.

Hundreds of satellites, some launched from the ground and some deployed from the shuttle, now keep constant watch on our home planet. They help us track and cope with the natural dangers that human beings have always faced, such as tropical storms and volcanic eruptions. They also give us evidence of a planet in trouble: vast areas of dying forest, shrinking ice caps, and holes in the ozone layer, which shields us from the Sun's deadly ultraviolet rays.

Space technology has given us images that show what Earth's wisest human beings have always taught: the precious resources of Earth are fragile and must be treated respectfully. As astronaut Jim Buchli put it, looking homeward from the shuttle window, "Look how thin the atmosphere is. Everything beyond that thin blue line is the void of space. And everything that we do to this environment, and our quality of life, is below that little blue line. That's the only difference between what we enjoy here on Earth and the really harsh, uninhabitable blackness of space."

Opposite page: *Almost one acre (half a hectare) of tropical rainforest is destroyed every second, wiping out unique animal and plant species before we can ever see and study them.*

HOT ROCKS

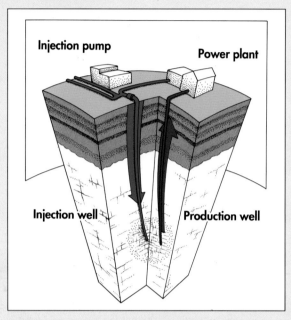

In the "hot-dry-rock energy system," cold water is pumped down one shaft (the injection well). It is heated by the rock bed and rises up a second shaft (the production well).

In a world where our fuel supplies are running low, or cost too much, or harm the environment, we dream of a cheap, safe, abundant source of energy. For many years, people in Hawaii, New Zealand, and Iceland have used hot springs to heat their homes and produce electricity. But most regions of the world don't have these "wet heat" sources. Today, scientists at an experimental site in New Mexico called Fenton Hill think they have found a new source of energy: hot rocks buried deep underground.

Geologists have long known that there is plenty of "dry heat" trapped in rock formations about three miles below the ground. The trick is to bring this heat to the surface so that we can use it.

The Fenton Hill team's plan was to drill a pair of shafts down to the hot rock. They would pump cold water down one shaft under pressure. When the rocks had heated it, the water would surge up the second shaft, all the way to the surface. The hot water could then be used to power turbines and generate electricity.

In 1986, the team built a working system and tested it for 30 days. They found that they could pump in water at 70°F (20°C) and get it back up to the surface 12 hours later, heated to 375°F (190°C). The only problem — and it was a big one — was that about a quarter of the water seeped away and was lost underground.

The research team is betting that if the system runs longer, the seeping water will form an underground reservoir, and then this water, too, can be pumped to the surface. Soon they will know for certain. During 1991 and 1992 the "hot-dry-rock" energy system, as it is called, is getting a longer test. Its supporters say it can already produce energy as cheaply as coal and nuclear power plants, and without their environmental problems. Maybe hot rocks will be cooking our food and running our computers sometime in the next century.

Twenty miles (30 kilometers) is not very far — about an hour's ride on a bicycle. But that distance is the upper limit to our living world. Just 20 miles above our heads, the air is too thin and too cold for us to survive. And just 60 miles (100 kilometers) beneath our feet — about an hour's drive by car — is an inferno of partly molten rock. Our whole living world exists on a thin crust of rock, wrapped in a fragile envelope of gases. Here you will find at least 400,000 different kinds of trees, shrubs, and grasses; at least 1,500,000 different kinds of crabs, spiders, scorpions, and insects; about 110,000 different kinds of snakes, clams, oysters, and octopuses; and about 45,000 kinds of fish, amphibians, reptiles, birds, and mammals. Human beings are just one mammal species on our Blue Planet, but we hold the fate of all the others — and perhaps the planet itself — in our hands.

Above: *Beetles come in more sizes, shapes, and kinds than any other insect group.*

Opposite page: *Broken by the tail fin of the space shuttle, the thin blue band in this view of Earth is our planet's atmosphere.*

EYES IN THE SKIES

Four Canadians, injured and exhausted, are stranded in northern Ontario bushland after their small plane crashes and sinks in a lake. An American weather satellite on its very first day of operation picks up their distress signal and fixes their position so they can be rescued.

Three young pilot whales, stranded on a Cape Cod beach, are nursed back to health and returned to the sea. Radio transmitters are attached to the three whales and monitored by satellite. Two of the devices fail, but one whale's transmitter holds up through 200,000 dives over a period of 95 days. By the time the battery wears out, this animal has safely joined a group of whales (called a pod), and biologists have a wealth of fresh information about pilot whale behavior.

An ancient Mayan city, complete with pyramid, has lain hidden in the dense Mexican rainforest for centuries.

Archaeologists recognize the site of the lost city on satellite images that show an area where jungle vegetation has been disturbed. Without the "map" provided by the satellite image, they would probably never have found it.

•

When the tiny satellite called *Explorer I* carried the United States into the space age in 1958, its Geiger counters detected the Van Allen belts of radiation, which encircle Earth. Since then, hundreds of satellites have been launched into orbit around our planet, sending vast quantities of information streaming back to receiving stations on Earth. Satellites, bristling with antennas, telescopes, cameras, and remote sensing devices, are helping us understand Earth's natural systems of air, water, and rock better than we ever have before. They have measured the slow movement of the continents and made images of the oceans, showing startling ridges and troughs under their smooth surfaces. More recently, a Nimbus 7 weather satellite provided the

TDRS — the Tracking and Data Relay Satellite — looks like two lacy parasols (dish antennas) connected to two giant flyswatters (arrays of solar panels).

first confirmation of the hole in the ozone layer over Antarctica, and the Upper Atmosphere Research Satellite (UARS), launched in 1991, studies how the ozone layer is thinning over all parts of the planet.

Before the 1960s, weather watchers had to gather information from many different ground weather stations to piece together a weather forecast. Now weather satellites make it possible to observe worldwide patterns of wind and cloud. They have also allowed us to tackle such weather mysteries as where and how hurricanes form, and what causes the strange Pacific Ocean warming known as El Niño, which changes weather patterns all over the world.

If there were a prize for most versatile satellite, Earth resources satellites called Landsats would probably win.

Landsats were first used to monitor the health of farm crops. But many branches of science have benefited from the information they record. They have discovered oil reserves in India, damage to Canadian forests from acid rain, and the breeding sites of desert locusts in Saudi Arabia. Their images have allowed some remote areas of the world to be mapped in detail for the first time. Even colonies of seals and penguins can be spotted and tracked from space.

Landsats now use a remote sensing instrument called the Thematic Mapper, which can detect amazingly fine details, including individual city streets. The measurements gathered by these satellites are processed by computers on the ground to make clear, usable images. A computer might, for example, enhance the contrast between different picture areas so that they can be seen more easily. Or different features might be assigned different colors so that they stand out. For instance, an image can be processed to show an oil slick

as a red patch on a black sea.

Satellites also allow human beings to communicate with each other over vast distances. In 1969, a newly linked network of communications satellites beamed Neil Armstrong's first step on the Moon to people all over the world. For the first time, satellites and television turned the world into a global village. Since then, communications satellites (called *comsats* for short) have become an everyday part of our lives, relaying messages from one part of the world to another.

TDRS (pronounced "tea-dress") is a communications satellite for other satellites. Two Tracking and Data Relay Satellites now collect data from other satellites and transmit them to Earth. Before TDRS, data had to be stored on satellites or the shuttle orbiter. It could be sent to Earth only during the brief periods when the spacecraft were "in view" of receiving stations on the ground. The first shuttle mission to use TDRS, in

1983, sent back more data in just seven days than all previous U.S. manned spaceflights combined. The TDRS system is so fast and powerful that it could

transmit the contents of a 20-volume encyclopedia — with 1,200 pages in each volume and 2,000 words on each page — in just a few seconds!

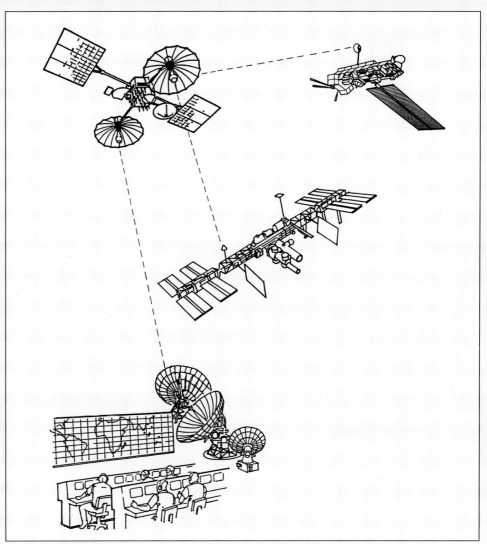

TDRS is the "satellite's satellite," gathering data from satellites and relaying them to receiving stations on Earth. It also relays information from the space shuttle and, in the future, from the space station.

THE UNQUIET EARTH

Surtsey leapt out of the waves like a mythical sea monster breathing fire. It was November 1963, and only a handful of people witnessed the birth of this tiny volcanic island off the coast of Iceland. On the first morning, clouds of black smoke rose from the sea. By evening, the onlookers spotted hardening lava just below the waves. By the second morning, a newly created piece of Earth's crust — later named Surtsey for the Icelandic god of fire — was rising out of the sea.

Churning, restless, and forever remaking itself: this is planet Earth. Although the ground seems solid beneath our feet, it is actually on the move. This movement goes on all the time and in every part of the world. Sometimes, when an earthquake shakes the ground or a volcano spews out molten rock, the movement is sudden and violent. But most of the time, Earth transforms itself so slowly that we cannot feel it or see it happening.

Our planet Earth is encased in a rocky crust, made mostly of basalt under the oceans and of granite under the continents. The thickness of this crust varies from about 25 miles (40 kilometers) under the Alps or the Himalayas to just three miles (five kilometers) under the sea. Beneath this thin crust is Earth's *mantle*, which is about 1,800 miles (2,900 kilometers) thick and continues all the way to Earth's core. The upper layer of the mantle is relatively rigid, but deeper in the mantle, the temperature is so hot that the rocks are softened and partly melted. The upper mantle and crust, which seem so solid to us, are actually sliding around on the softer layer underneath.

The crust does not move as one unit. Instead, it is broken into many jagged pieces, like the cracked shell of a hardboiled egg. These pieces are called *tectonic plates*. There are seven very large plates, with a number of smaller ones wedged in here and there. Six of these large plates include all or part of a continent and some of its surrounding waters. The seventh large plate lies entirely under the Pacific Ocean.

All of the tectonic plates are on the move, like immensely huge, slow rafts on a sluggish sea. The plates with continents on them travel about three quarters of an inch (two centimeters) in a year, while the ones entirely underwater shift as much as five inches (15 centimeters). Yet, over hundreds of millions of years, this creeping movement has smashed continents together and ripped them apart. Vast seas have formed and teemed with life, later becoming landlocked and gradually shrinking to nothing. Mountain ranges have been wrenched out of the ground in one place, while deep rifts yawned open somewhere else. This process of creation and destruction still goes on today. The tectonic plates are Earth's massive recycling system for its rocks and minerals.

Areas where plates are moving away from each other are called *spreading zones*. They are usually found

Above: *This dramatic mural by Peter Sawyer shows the erupting volcanoes that dotted the Earth's surface three and a half billion years ago. Geologic forces still at work today were shaping the Earth, while early life forms were first emerging.*

Opposite page: *The Sinai peninsula is isolated by two spreading zones as Africa breaks away from Asia.*

beneath the oceans. Molten rock, called *magma*, wells up from Earth's mantle to fill in the rift that opens as the plates move apart. As the magma hardens and builds up, it forms a mountain ridge — with a rift valley at its summit — on the ocean floor. In fact, the greatest mountain range on Earth is not the Andes, or even the Himalayas, but a 25,000-mile (40,000-kilometer) chain of mountains called the Mid-Ocean Ridge, which forms great snaking loops around the world under the oceans. Looming unseen, the ridge marks plate boundaries where new crust is being created.

The 10,000-mile (16,000-kilometer) portion called the Mid-Atlantic Ridge follows the boundaries between the North and South American plates on one side and the Eurasian and African plates on the other. The spreading boundary line, where magma is rising, is studded with live volcanoes. Sometimes, like Iceland (and little Surtsey), these volcanoes rise above the ocean to form islands.

There is only so much surface area for Earth's plates to occupy. If two plates are pushing away from each other, growing along their edges as new crust builds up, then somewhere else plates must be getting smaller. This shrinkage occurs in a *subduction zone*, where two plates are colliding. (But remember, this slow, grinding "collision" takes place over millions of years.) When two plates collide, the denser one may slide under the other. The leading edge

Opposite page: A ground view of the Sakurajima volcano in Japan. This volcano has been active since 1955 and has been "smoking" like this for several years. The shuttle astronauts can spot it from space.

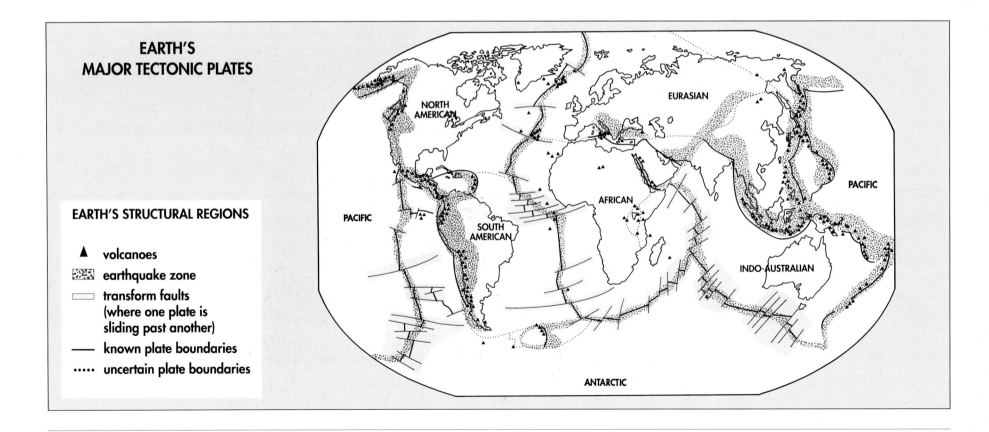

EARTH'S MAJOR TECTONIC PLATES

EARTH'S STRUCTURAL REGIONS

▲ volcanoes
▨ earthquake zone
▢ transform faults (where one plate is sliding past another)
— known plate boundaries
····· uncertain plate boundaries

NORTH AMERICAN
EURASIAN
PACIFIC
PACIFIC
AFRICAN
SOUTH AMERICAN
INDO-AUSTRALIAN
ANTARCTIC

BLACK SMOKERS AND OTHER WONDERS

In the late 1970s, a group of scientists were exploring an undersea mountain ridge off the Pacific Coast of Mexico. As *Alvin*, their tiny deep-sea research submersible, reached a depth of 8,500 feet (2,500 meters), they peered in amazement from its windows. In the glow of *Alvin*'s floodlights, they saw an eerie landscape. It was strewn with craggy rock "chimneys" puffing out dark clouds that looked like smoke. The clouds turned out to be superheated water (sometimes as hot as 600°F/ 300°C), billowing into the cold ocean.

Where does this water come from? It is seawater that has seeped down through cracks in the undersea plates until it reaches hot magma. When the magma has heated the water to scalding temperatures, it erupts out of the ocean floor again, bringing dissolved minerals with it. These minerals — mostly iron, zinc, and copper sulfides — give the clouds their dark color, and their nickname: "black smokers." The minerals harden when they hit cold seawater. Gradually, they form the chimneys, new pieces of Earth's crust recycled from the mantle. Black smokers and other superheated geysers have now been found on several other undersea mountain ridges, including one northeast of the Galapagos Islands.

With these discoveries has come another unexpected treasure. A foul-smelling gas called hydrogen sulfide belches out of the seabed along with the hot water. Thick mats of bacteria that live on this gas coat the surrounding rocks. They, in turn, provide food for an amazing array of creatures: waving clusters of seaworms up to ten feet (three meters) long, jellyfish that look like many-petaled flowers, clams as big as footballs, and blind, scuttling crabs. Until they were seen, no one had any idea such creatures could exist in the black depths of the ocean. One awed scientist said that it was like discovering a new continent with all its unknown plants and animals.

Small maneuverable subs like Alvin *have finally allowed us to explore the least-known parts of our planet — the deep ocean floors.*

of the sinking plate, carrying crust with it, melts as it is drawn down, or *subducted,* into the hotter, deeper parts of the mantle. In this way, rock that was once part of Earth's crust becomes part of its molten insides. The deepest seafloor in the world, 36,000 feet (11,000 meters) below the waves, is the Marianas Trench in the Pacific Ocean. This is where the Pacific plate plunges down as it slides under the smaller Philippine plate.

If two continents are brought together by colliding plates, the enormous pressure may crumple the land into huge mountain ranges. (Imagine moving a heavy piece of furniture that pushes the carpet into rippling folds.) The Himalayas, for instance, were created when India, on the Indo-Australian plate, rammed into the Eurasian plate.

Sometimes, instead of colliding, plates grind slowly past each other. For instance, the Pacific plate is moving northward past the North American plate. At times, sections of the plates snag each other and lock. The pressure builds until one suddenly breaks free and lurches forward, causing an earthquake.

Scientists think that Earth's plates have been on the move for about 2.5 billion years. If the plates moved at an average of two and a half inches (six centimeters) a year, they could have circled Earth four times during this immense period. The continents have probably collided and parted several times and have traveled far from their present sites. For instance, there is geological evidence that Antarctica and Africa's Sahara Desert were covered by the same dome of

Opposite page: *The lights of an undersea submersible pick up a crab scuttling across its strange deep-sea home—a "black smoker" some 8,500 feet (2,500 meters) below the surface of the ocean.*

STILL LOOKING FOR PANGAEA?

The green sea turtles that live off the coast of Brazil usually lead placid lives, grazing on sea grass. But every two or three years they begin an epic journey. With their strong flippers cutting through the waves like a seabird's wings through the air, the turtles swim nearly halfway across the Atlantic Ocean — an epic journey of 1,400 miles

The strong flippers of a green sea turtle cut smoothly through the water in this painting by Lloyd E. Logan.

(2,200 kilometers). When they reach the tiny island of Ascension, they mate and the females lay their eggs in the sand.

Biologists have long wondered how the turtles can find Ascension. Some suggest that the turtles have a kind of natural compass that helps them to navigate the route. Others think the turtles may be able to find their way by the smell or taste of Ascension, carried by ocean currents. But even more baffling than how they do it, is why they do it. Why take the risk of such a long journey?

Maybe the answer lies in the breakup of southern Pangaea, where these turtles once lived. As a rift opened up between South America and Africa about 100 million years ago, a chain of volcanic islands may have formed in the waters between them. Turtles like to lay their eggs on offshore islands to protect them from predators. Perhaps they got into the habit of swimming out to the nearest, oldest island. But as the rift got wider, the oldest island was carried away from the volcanic hot spot that brought it to life. When it sank under the waves, the turtles had to swim to the next island in the chain, a little farther away. Over millions of years, as old islands died and new islands formed, the turtles had to swim farther and farther. Perhaps the stubborn creatures were slowly lured out to the middle of the ocean to find a safe haven for their eggs.

ice 450 million years ago. More recently, a mere 250 million years ago, all of Earth's land masses seem to have been joined together in one supercontinent dubbed Pangaea, which was surrounded by one great ocean. When dinosaurs first appeared on Earth, all Pangaea was theirs to roam. Then, slowly, the land began to break apart again.

The portion holding North America and Eurasia moved north and gradually, over millions of years, split in two. Gondwana, the remaining land mass in the south, split to become South America, Africa, Antarctica, Australia — and India, far away from its present home. If you look at the globe, it is still easy to imagine how the east coast of South America and the west coast of Africa were joined 135 million years ago, with present-day Brazil nestled under the "shoulder" of West Africa. About 100 million years ago, India began a stately journey north, which took 80 million years to complete, to reach its present position.

If Earth's tectonic plates keep moving for another 100 million years at the same pace they're moving now, there will be many changes in the planet we know. As Africa butts against Eurasia, the Mediterranean (which is already shrinking) will disappear. Africa's Great Rift Valley will break apart to form a seaway. Australia will be heading north for a rendezvous with Southeast Asia. The Pacific will be much narrower, and the Atlantic will be much wider. And sometime even further into the future, perhaps 250 million years from now, all the land on Earth may once again unite to form a new Pangaea.

Opposite page: *The Mediterranean Sea, with the Atlantic in the foreground, Portugal to the left, and Africa to the right — Gibraltar in the center.*

The highly cratered far side of the Moon records the intense bombardment history of the early solar system.

IMPACT!

The battered surface of the Moon bears the scars of every fight it ever had with other chunks of the universe. You can see the largest craters with your own eyes — they form the face of the "Man in the Moon." Unlike Earth, the Moon has no water, no atmosphere, and no moving plates to smooth out signs of impact. Because our planet has all these things, most of its impact scars have been erased. However, the Barringer Crater in Arizona still looks like what it is — the place where a meteorite about 100 feet (30 meters) across plowed into our planet some 50,000 years ago. It gouged out a hole 4,000 feet (1,200 meters) wide and 600 feet (180 meters) deep. If the crater were used as a stadium, it could hold about two and a half million people!

Earth has impact craters more than 50 times larger than this, but their outlines have been blurred over time. One of the oldest is Canada's Sudbury Basin, 40 miles (60 kilometers) long and 20 miles (30 kilometers) wide. Almost two billion years ago, an asteroid slammed into Earth here, bringing a treasure trove with it — one of the world's richest lodes of nickel, cobalt, and platinum ores.

Did another asteroid — perhaps six miles (ten kilometers) across, weighing perhaps a trillion tons — doom the dinosaurs some 65 million years ago? Scientists are still debating this subject. If an object this massive struck Earth, it could cause devastating tidal waves and fire storms. Clouds of dust in the atmosphere would block out sunlight, killing plants on land and in the sea. Any animals that survived the impact would die of cold and starvation. There is mounting geological evidence that something catastrophic happened on Earth at about the time the dinosaurs disappeared. But if it *was* an asteroid, where is its impact crater? It may have been recycled into the Earth's crust and lost forever. However, new evidence points to an impact crater in Mexico, and scientists are studying it closely.

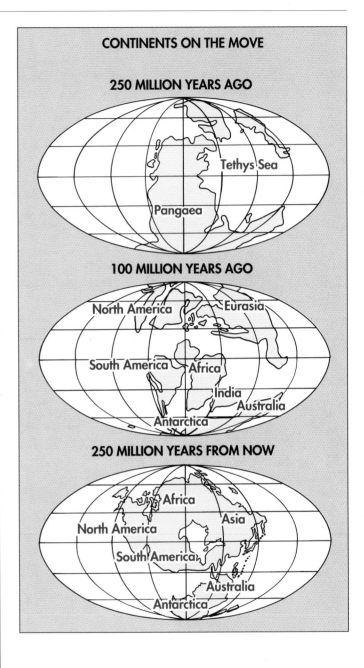

CONTINENTS ON THE MOVE

250 MILLION YEARS AGO

Tethys Sea

Pangaea

100 MILLION YEARS AGO

North America

Eurasia

South America

Africa

India

Australia

Antarctica

250 MILLION YEARS FROM NOW

Africa

North America

Asia

South America

Australia

Antarctica

Opposite page: *The Barringer Crater in Arizona, formed about 50,000 years ago when a meteorite collided with the Earth.*

MOUNTAINS OF FIRE

A powerful volcanic eruption seems like the end of the world for people caught in its path. In 79 A.D., the Roman city of Pompeii suffocated under 20 feet (six meters) of choking ash that rained down from Mount Vesuvius. In 1902, Saint Pierre, Martinique, was engulfed by a cloud of scorching gases that swept down from Mount Pelée at more than 100 mph (160 km/h). The town was leveled, and out of its 28,000 inhabitants, only two people survived — one of them a prisoner in a thick-walled jail. In 1985, the eruption of Nevado del Ruiz in Colombia sent a torrent of steaming mud crashing down on the town of Armero. Twenty-two thousand people were killed.

In some of the greatest vol-

canic cataclysms we know of — Tambora in 1815 and Krakatoa in 1883 — entire Indonesian islands were ripped apart, producing mountainous waves, called *tsunamis*, that drowned thousands of people. The eruption of Krakatoa was 26 times as powerful as the largest hydrogen bomb ever tested. The explosion also produced the loudest sound ever recorded, heard 3,000 miles (4,800 kilometers) away!

Many scientists believe volcanoes that discharge huge amounts of ash into the high atmosphere can change the world's weather by blocking out sunlight. Tambora's violent explosion may have caused the "year without a summer" in 1816. During that summer, snow fell in the northeastern United States and in London, England. Mary Shelley, vacationing beside Lake Geneva, Switzerland, found it so cold outdoors that she stayed inside

— and wrote *Frankenstein.*

Today there are about 600 "active" volcanoes on land (and hundreds more under the oceans). A volcano is considered active if it has erupted within the past few hundred years and dormant (asleep) if it last erupted within the past several thousand years. Every region of the world has active volcanoes, even Antarctica. But about three-quarters of the world's active volcanoes are in the "Ring of Fire" circling the Pacific from New Zealand to Southeast Asia to Japan, and from Alaska to California to South America.

This danger zone is caused by the Pacific Plate grinding against all the plates around it and gradually sliding under them. As the plate's leading edge sinks down into the mantle, it melts. Some of this molten rock forms an underground reservoir called a magma chamber. Seething with trapped steam and other gases, the magma is under immense pressure from the surrounding rocks. It begins to force its way upward through cracks in the rocks, triggering hundreds of small earthquakes. As the earth shifts and splits, some of the magma finds its way to the surface as lava. Repeated eruptions slowly build up a cone-shaped mountain. From time to time, the magma chamber fills up with its explosive mix of water, gas, and molten rock, and the volcano erupts.

Some of the most dangerous eruptions occur when the pathway to the outside is blocked by debris from previous eruptions. Enormous pressure can build up inside the volcano. When the explosion finally comes, the whole top of the mountain may blow off. This is what happened in 1980 to Mount Saint Helens, which ejected 275 million tons of pent-up material into the air — about one ton for every American!

Some volcanoes form over "hot spots." These are holes in the crust that go all the way down to the molten mantle. Hot spots stay in one place while the plates move slowly over them, creating chains of volcanic islands. This is how the Hawaiian Islands were formed. At the southeast end

of the chain, the newest volcano, Loihi, can be seen rising from the ocean floor. In about 100,000 years, Loihi will form a new Hawaiian Island.

Hot spot volcanoes usually erupt more often but less violently than plate boundary volcanoes. This makes them easier to study. In fact, Kilauea, on Hawaii's Big Island, is probably the world's most watched volcano. Volcanologists, wearing fireproof suits and gas masks,

A lava fountain erupting and flowing away from Kilauea on the Big Island of Hawaii in 1986. The Hawaiian hot spot has been supplying magma for more than 70 million years to a line of volcanoes stretching from Hawaii to the Aleutian Islands.

venture close to the lava flows and steaming vents. They measure lava temperature and collect samples of the foul-smelling poisonous gases the volcano is belching out. They also install instruments to monitor the volcano from a safer distance. Seismographs register the many small earthquakes caused by rising magma. Tiltmeters (rather like carpenter's levels) and laser telemeters measure tiny changes in the volcano's slopes

as magma makes them shift and bulge. Scientists are getting much better at predicting when an eruption is likely to occur, so that people can be evacuated. But it is still very hard to predict whether a volcano will mutter or whether it will roar.

Billions of years ago, steam and gas erupting from volcanoes may have provided early planet Earth with water and air. As the early crust of Earth recycled itself, a wealth of minerals such as copper, gold, silver, and tin were brought to the surface. More than 80 percent of Earth's crust as we know it today has been formed by volcanic activity of one kind or another.

Volcanoes build mountains and form new islands. Volcanic ash makes soil very fertile, which is why farmers continue to plant the slopes of the world's most dangerous volcanoes. Just a few weeks after Mount Saint Helens erupted, grasses and flowers began to grow again on its shattered slopes. In spite of the short-term destruction they bring to people, volcanoes are a creative force in the world, recycling material from deep inside Earth.

WHEN THE GROUND SHAKES

On the evening of October 17, 1989, people all over North America had settled down in front of their TV sets to watch a World Series baseball game. They got something else instead — live coverage of a powerful earthquake that shook San Francisco and communities to the south.

For the hundreds who were hurt or killed, and for those whose homes or businesses were destroyed, the Loma Prieta quake was a tragedy. Overall, though, Northern Californians were very lucky. They live in an area where most houses and offices are sturdily built to withstand earthquakes. In contrast, in 1988, an earthquake in Soviet Armenia killed about 25,000 people. Many of them lived in flimsy apartment blocks that collapsed into rubble.

•

There are about a million earthquakes in the world every year. They range from tiny

The Marina District of San Francisco — built on landfill — was hard hit by the Loma Prieta Earthquake of October 1989. Some houses were so badly damaged that they had to be torn down. People who had lived in them were allowed just 15 minutes inside to collect what they could before the houses were demolished.

tremors that hardly rattle a teacup to massive quakes that level cities and kill hundreds or even thousands of people. In ancient times, people of many lands believed that Earth was carried on the back of an animal — an ox, a tortoise, a catfish, even a snake. When the animal shifted its burden, the ground shook. Now we know that the restless creature is Earth itself.

Ninety percent of earth-quakes occur on the ragged boundaries of the tectonic plates, especially in the "Ring of Fire" around the Pacific Ocean. Plates trying to slide under or past another plate get snagged at some point. Then suddenly the "locked" plate breaks free and lurches forward. This sudden, violent burst of energy causes shock waves to rush out in all directions, at speeds up to 18,000 mph (29,000 km/h). The fastest are called P (for *primary*) waves. They cause rock to compress (shrink) and then expand again. The 1964 Alaska earthquake was first felt in Anchorage as a sharp thud caused by P waves. This was strong enough to stop people in their tracks. After a couple of seconds, the slightly slower S (for *secondary*) waves hit, causing the ground to shake from side to side. But the real devastation was still to come.

Almost always, the worst

earthquake damage is caused by the slowest waves, which travel along the surface of Earth. For more than three minutes during the Alaska quake, surface waves caused the ground to heave in long, sickening rolls. People were thrown to the ground, where they lay terrified and helpless. The pavements cracked open, and shops, restaurants, and office buildings collapsed into their basements. Landslides triggered by the quake swept away whole streets of houses.

This earthquake was one of the most powerful in history, measured at 8.5 on the Richter scale. This scale, developed in 1935 by Charles Richter of the California Institute of Technology, measures the *magnitude*, or size, of the shock waves produced by an earthquake. Each whole number, moving up the scale, represents ten times the ground motion and about 30 times the energy release of the previous number. So the Great San Francisco Earthquake of 1906, estimated at 8.3, shook the ground more than ten times as powerfully as the 1989 Loma Prieta Earthquake, measured at 7.1.

For centuries, people in earthquake zones have been on the lookout for early signs of trouble. Horses whinnying and stamping, mice and rats fleeing their nests, cloudy or bubbling well water, rotten-egg stenches, and little tremors in the ground have all been mentioned as warnings of major quakes about to happen. In 1975, after signs like these, the city of Haicheng, China, was evacuated in time to save its people from a major quake.

The most common way of predicting earthquake risk is to look closely at the known weak places, or "faults," in the Earth's crust. Scientists gather evidence from written historical records and the land itself. Then they try to find a pattern in past earthquakes. Along the San Andreas fault line in California, for example, the places where no movement has occurred for a long time are probably under the greatest stress. There is a good chance that a southern part of the fault, which has not had a large quake since 1857, will

In 1906, hundreds of San Francisco buildings tumbled in a severe earthquake. A raging fire followed, destroying much of the city.

have a 7.5 or greater earthquake in the next 30 years. This is useful knowledge in some ways — communities at risk can work on their emergency plans, and they can develop tough building codes to make buildings as sturdy as possible. But people cannot change their daily lives for 30 years while waiting for "the big one."

By the end of this century, the Earth Orbiting System, a joint project of NASA (National Aeronautics and Space Administration) and the European Space Agency, may lend help from space. Orbiting space platforms will measure the worldwide movements of Earth's plates and relay these measurements to the ground, where scientists will be able to monitor plate shifts as they occur. Someday this may help them predict where the next pressure point will build and break.

THE WEATHER MACHINE

In less than ten thundering minutes, the space shuttle zooms into orbit, about 250 miles (400 kilometers) from Earth. In that short time, the astronauts leave behind everything that makes life on Earth possible: air to breathe, water, warmth, and protection from the sun's deadliest rays. When the space travelers look back toward Earth, they see a planet where these things are provided naturally. They see reflected sunlight, billowing clouds driven by Earth's winds, and plentiful water. These are just the visible parts of Earth's weather machine — a never-ending heating and cooling of Earth's surface, and a never-ending cycling of air and water over the face of the planet. The energy that powers the weather machine comes from 93 million miles (150 million kilometers) away, from the star we call the Sun.

Above: Benjamin Franklin's famous (and dangerous) kite experiment proved that lightning was a form of electricity.

Left: Clouds and a river take part in the endless recycling of Earth's water. Clouds are formed when water evaporates, rises into the air, and condenses (turns back into water droplets) on bits of dust or sea salt. Soon these droplets fall to Earth again as rain.

Opposite page: The sinister cloudy pinwheel of Typhoon Sam (1989). Spiraling storms in the South Pacific region are called typhoons, while the same type of storms over the Atlantic are called hurricanes.

THE CLOUD NETS AT CHUNGUNGO, CHILE

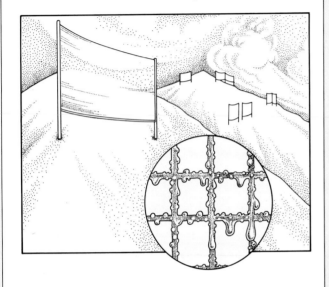

CATCHING CLOUDS IN A NET

They look like giant volleyball nets, 50 of them, scattered on an arid hilltop in northern Chile. But these inexpensive polypropylene meshes, each 45 feet long and 13 feet high (14 meters by 4 meters) work magic for the people of Chungungo. This is a little fishing village, called a *caleta*, at the bottom of the hills. The caleta is in one of the driest regions on Earth, where the total rainfall for the whole year is barely enough to dampen the ground. Low-lying clouds, heavily laden with water, often drift in from the Pacific Ocean and pass right over the village. These clouds never drop their water as rain. But as they travel inland, they form a thick fog on the hilltops.

For many years, the people of Chungungo were forced to use expensive, trucked-in water. But now a team of Chileans, working with Dr. Robert Schemenauer from Canada, has set up hilltop nets to capture the precious cloud water. As the clouds flow through the nets, tiny beads of water are left behind on the mesh. The droplets run together and flow down the strands into a trough, and then into a network of pipes. The nets collect about 1,800 gallons (7,000 liters) of drinkable water a day. This gives villagers five and a half gallons (22 liters) of water per person per day, twice what they had before. Even so, this is a very small amount of water for all their daily needs, which include bathing, cooking, and washing clothes, as well as the need for drinking water. (The average North American uses about 15 times as much water in a day.)

A pipeline from the hilltop will soon be completed. Then the villagers will have cloud water piped directly into their homes — the first water system of this type in the world. Similar projects are now under way in arid coastal areas of Peru and Oman. People lucky enough to live where the conditions are right can now have a clean, dependable water supply. And it will keep on flowing as long as clouds form over the oceans of our planet.

The Sun is a huge, churning ball of gases. Nuclear reactions deep inside the Sun cause it to radiate enormous amounts of energy. Earth receives only about one part in two billion of this energy. Some of this is immediately reflected back into space by Earth's atmosphere, clouds, and light-colored areas of snow or sand. But some of it is absorbed by our oceans and land. As Earth's surface is warmed, it radiates (sends out) heat. The atmosphere keeps this heat from escaping into space, in much the same way a blanket traps your body heat and keeps you warm.

The Sun's energy doesn't reach all parts of Earth equally. The Sun's rays strike the North and South poles at a much greater angle than they strike the equator (Earth's "waistline"). In addition, polar snow and ice reflect a lot of sunlight instead of absorbing it. For these reasons, the polar regions are much colder than the tropics, the area near the equator.

If you take a look at a globe, you will see that it

Above: *Towering cumulus clouds in New Mexico form a natural laboratory for studying atmospheric conditions.*

Opposite page: *The awesome energy release of a lightning strike, photographed in New Mexico.*

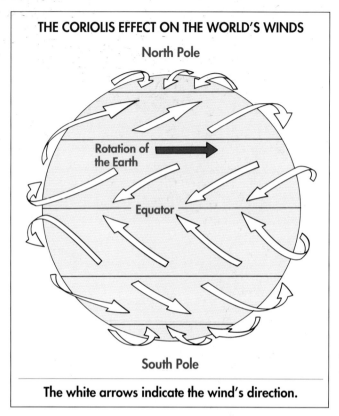

THE CORIOLIS EFFECT ON THE WORLD'S WINDS

North Pole

Rotation of the Earth

Equator

South Pole

The white arrows indicate the wind's direction.

Opposite page: Hurricane Hugo hit South Carolina with devastating force in 1989. It left some strange debris behind, including this heavy dining table, left marooned in a tree as floodwaters receded.

is held in its frame at an angle. This is to show how Earth is tipped as it revolves around the Sun. For half the year, the Northern Hemisphere is tilted toward the Sun. It receives more heat at this time and has its summer. For the other half of the year, the Northern Hemisphere is tilted away from the Sun and has its winter. In the Southern Hemisphere, things are reversed, so Australia is having its winter when North America is having its summer.

These differences in temperature between one part of Earth and another bring about the daily changes in cloud cover, wind, rain, and snow that we call weather. It is this heating and cooling, caused by the Sun, that sets the atmosphere in motion. Wind is simply Earth's atmosphere on the move, sweeping along with it the clouds that sometimes bring us drizzle, downpours, hailstorms, and blizzards.

The part of Earth's atmosphere closest to the surface is a breathable mixture of nitrogen, oxygen, carbon dioxide, water vapor, and other gases that we call air. When all these gases in the air are heated by the Sun's energy, they expand (spread out), and begin to rise. This rising and spreading reduces the pressure of the air. An area where warm air is rising is therefore called a low pressure area. Colder, heavier air rushes toward low pressure areas to replace the warm air that rose. Where cold, heavy air is slowly sinking, increasing the pressure of the air, a high pressure area forms.

Since the equatorial region is the hottest place on Earth, warm air rises there. Cooler air blows in from north and south to take the place of the rising air. Instead of blowing straight at the equator, however, these winds blow at an angle. This is caused by the rotation of our planet. The surface of Earth at the equator is furthest from the axis of rotation, so it moves from west to east faster than the surface at higher latitudes. Air moving toward the equator therefore tends to veer westward, while air moving away from the equator tends to veer eastward. This is called the *Coriolis effect.*

The resulting *trade winds* in the Northern Hemisphere blow from northeast to southwest. In the Southern Hemisphere, they blow from southeast to northwest. The Coriolis effect also causes low-pressure storm systems in the Northern Hemisphere to rotate with counterclockwise circulation, while those in the Southern Hemisphere rotate in the clockwise direction.

Some winds may blow in only one part of the world or at only one time of the year. Monsoons are probably the best known seasonal winds in the weather machine. Large bodies of water heat up and cool down much more slowly than land. During the winter, India becomes cooler than the Indian Ocean to the south. A high pressure area forms over the land, and dry winds blow across India toward the sea. During the summer, though, India becomes hotter than the ocean. A cool wind blows from the Indian Ocean, northward across India. This is the summer monsoon, carrying heavy rain with it. About half the world's people — in China, the countries of South-East Asia, and some countries in Africa — depend on monsoons to water their crops.

FROZEN IN TIME

Science fiction movies and books have often told of amazing — and sometimes terrifying — discoveries in the polar ice: alien spaceships, prehistoric men, or nightmarish "creatures" are found deep frozen and are then thawed by curious human beings. In real life, hundreds of mammoths, which died out about 10,000 years ago, have been found in the ice of Siberia. They are perfectly preserved, with woolly coats, tusks, and the still-fresh remains of their last meal in their stomachs. But did you know that Arctic and Antarctic ice itself tells a dramatic story of Earth's early history?

The Hubbard Glacier in Alaska, one of the last remains of an Ice Age that ended about 10,000 years ago.

The great polar ice sheets built up in layers, year after year. Teams of researchers have drilled solid cores of ice from these ice sheets. On these ice cores — drilled as much as one mile (1.6 kilometers) deep — scientists can count and analyze the yearly layers like tree rings. For Greenland, we already have a year-by-year ice record going back 100,000 years. A drilling project now under way in Antarctica will eventually bore out half a million years of ice history.

Studying these ice cores is a reminder that everything in our world is interconnected. Ash from the eruption of Krakatoa in 1883 has been found layered in faraway Antarctic ice. And from more recent years, radioactive dust in the ice traces the history of above-ground nuclear testing.

The buried ice layers contain bubbles of atmosphere trapped when the layers were formed. Scientists can measure how much carbon dioxide and other "greenhouse gases" were in the air during the past. From the detailed composition of the ice itself, they can also estimate the temperature when the snow originally fell. It turns out that as far back as the ice record goes, carbon dioxide levels were always higher in warm periods and lower in cold ones. This is a powerful warning. Human beings, with their cars and their industries, are now pumping huge amounts of carbon dioxide into the atmosphere. We may already be warming the planet, with long-term results we can only begin to imagine.

Some of the most dreaded winds, blowing at up to 200 mph (320 km/h), are found in hurricanes. From space, hurricanes look like pinwheels. This is because the Coriolis effect puts a spin on the winds rushing toward the center (the "eye") of the hurricane. The center is, as you would expect, a very low pressure area. Hurricanes are born in the Atlantic Ocean near the equator, where about a hundred pinwheels start to take shape each year. But only about six become mature hurricanes, heading northwest toward the West Indies and the east coast of North America.

The weather machine also recycles Earth's water supply. For at least three billion years, Earth has been recycling the same water supply, over and over again. The rain that falls on your head might once have rolled down a dinosaur's scaly back. Over 90 percent of our water is in the oceans. Only a little more than three percent is fresh water. Most of this is stored in the polar ice caps or is buried groundwater. Less than one percent is in lakes, rivers, and streams. And less than half of one percent is in the atmosphere at any one time.

When water is heated, its molecules bounce around in all directions. Some of them leap right into the air and evaporate, which means that they become an odorless, invisible gas called water vapor. When the Sun shines on a puddle and "dries it up," the water hasn't disappeared from the water cycle. It has simply changed its state from liquid to gas.

Most of the water vapor in our atmosphere comes

Opposite page: The Brazilian rainforest in the midst of a downpour. We have learned that rainforests actually produce their own weather, since evaporation of water from rainforest plants and soil accounts for up to half the water that falls back down on them.

from the oceans. When the Sun shines on the oceans, a small amount of their water evaporates. However, some water vapor in the air comes from living things. Rainforest trees and other plants breathe out, or transpire, huge amounts of water vapor.

The warmer the air is, the more water vapor it can hold. As warm air rises, it carries the water vapor up with it. Eventually it meets colder air. Cold air can't hold as much water vapor as warm air, so some of the water vapor turns back into water droplets. It condenses on particles of dust or salt to form clouds. Eventually the water falls from the clouds again as rain, hail, or snow.

For the last few hundred years, people have used weather instruments to gather accurate information about rainfall, temperature, and other weather conditions. For a few thousand years before that, we have the notes people sometimes wrote about storms, droughts, and floods they had seen. To check back any further, we have to look at nature's record: the yearly patterns of tree rings, ice cores (see p. 32), and the marks of long-ago weather etched in rocks. From all these clues, we have built up a history of our planet's climate. Climate is simply the usual patterns of weather over a period of time.

We have learned that Earth has gone through great climatic changes. The dinosaurs of 100 million years ago basked in much warmer temperatures than we have today. Twenty thousand years ago, human beings huddled in caves while great ice sheets covered much of North America and northern Europe. The causes of these great swings in climate — and the smaller changes in between — are still under study. We do know that one cause of climatic swings lies in the slow changes in the way Earth orbits the Sun. The Earth's axis wobbles like that of a spinning top, and the angle at which Earth is tilted as well as the roundness of Earth's orbit also change through time. Together, these astronomical effects appear to turn the ice ages on and off. We know, too, that during warmer periods there has been more carbon dioxide in the atmosphere. But we are not yet sure how our planet regulates the amounts.

Climatic change is of great concern to us. For about the last 200 years, Earth has been getting warmer. And, for the first time in the planet's four-and-a-half-billion-year history, human beings themselves are changing the gases in Earth's atmosphere. It is a race against time to limit these changes and to find out as much as we can about how we are affecting our planet's natural recycling systems.

Left: *This detail from a painting by John Gurche shows a range of ancient creatures, including four dinosaurs in the background, which lived at different times tens of millions of years ago. The largest animals who ever lived, dinosaurs dominated Earth for some 140 million years.*

Opposite page: *From the space shuttle, the effects of Earth's winds on this desert landscape are clearly visible. These mountainous sand dunes are in the Namib Desert on the Atlantic coast of Namibia in southwest Africa.*

LOOK WHAT WE'VE DONE TO OUR AIR

Have you heard the story of the sorcerer's apprentice? He used a magic spell to turn brooms into slaves who would do his work for him. But he didn't know the spell to stop them, and their mindless work turned into a rampage. So it is with the fossil fuels we burn in our factories, cars, and planes, and the pollutants they produce. And so it is with many of the chemical compounds we have invented. Carried high up into the atmosphere or blown from one country to another on the winds, these substances have destructive powers that we did not foresee and now find difficult to control. We are changing Earth's atmosphere faster than it has ever changed before. And although we are finally starting to clean things up, we have already damaged our planet in ways that will take a long time to heal.

•

Acid Rain

Acid rain is just as sinister as it sounds. It has bitten into the stone of castles, churches, and other historic buildings all over Europe. It has clouded the brilliant stained glass of cathedral windows. Because of acid rain and other pollution, ancient Greek temples have crumbled more in the last 25 years than in the 2,400 years before that. Thousands of lakes in the northeastern United States and central Canada are so acidic that no fish can survive in them. All over Europe and in many parts of North America, whole forests are dying, probably because of acid rain.

Acid rain is caused mainly by sulfur and nitrogen. They are added to the air when fossil fuels such as coal and oil are burned by industry and by car engines. These pollutants join with water in the air to make nitric acid and sulfuric acid, which then fall to the ground mixed with rain or snow.

Acid rain is measured on the pH scale, where battery acid has

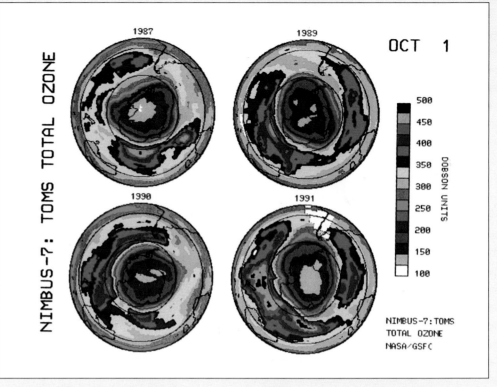

A series of images from a Nimbus 7 weather satellite show the "hole" in the ozone layer as a pink and purple area over Antarctica. The measurements used to produce these false color computer images were made in October of 1987, '89, '90 and '91. In those years, ozone was measured at 120 to 125 Dobson units (the standard ozone measuring unit), much lower than the 220 Dobson units of ozone in this region before CFCs began to eat into it. Scientists calculate that this ozone loss allows twice as much of the Sun's harmful ultraviolet radiation to reach Earth.

a pH of one and milk has a pH of six. Eastern North America often has rainfalls and snowfalls rated at pH three and a half or lower (about the same acidity as lemon juice), and rain rated at two on the pH scale (as acidic as vinegar) has sometimes fallen in Pennsylvania.

In 1985, 21 countries, including Canada and most European countries, signed an agreement to reduce their sulfur dioxide pollution by 30 percent by 1993. Since then, the European Community countries have gone further, pledging to reduce sulfur dioxide emissions

A choking smog blankets Los Angeles, which, like many of the world's large cities, has severe air pollution problems. Los Angeles is planning tough restrictions on car design and use in an effort to clean up its air.

by 60 percent by 2003, and nitrogen oxide emissions by 30 percent by 1998. Even the United States and Britain, which have long resisted signing any acid rain agreements, are finally taking action. However, environmentalists advise that sulfur dioxide emissions should be cut by 90 percent. Until that happens, lakes will continue to die, and historic buildings will continue to crumble.

•

The Hole in the Ozone Layer

Have you ever noticed a crisp tang in the air after a thunderstorm? You are getting a tiny whiff of ozone, released by lightning strikes. Ozone, a form of oxygen, plays a strange role in our lives. At ground level, coughed out by cars and factories, ozone is a pollutant. It is also one of the ingredients in smog and acid rain, and in large enough quantities, it is poisonous. But about ten miles (15 kilometers) from Earth, ozone is a lifesaver. Although this part of the atmosphere is called the ozone layer, the ozone is thinly spread — only a few molecules for every million molecules of air. But this small amount of ozone filters out some of the Sun's harmful ultraviolet rays before they can reach us. These are the rays that cause sunburn and, worse, skin cancer and eye cataracts.

The greatest danger to the ozone layer comes from chemicals called chlorofluorocarbons (CFCs). For a long time, these chemicals have been used as coolants in refrigerators and air conditioners. They are also used to blow up the foam for styrofoam containers, and to enable furniture polish, hairspray, and pesticides to spray out of cans.

The trouble comes when CFCs drift up into the stratosphere. There, they break down and release chlorine. The chlorine reacts with the ozone and turns it into oxygen, which can't block ultraviolet radiation. The chlorine itself does not change: it makes the chemical reaction happen without becoming part of it. So every molecule of chlorine is free to go on destroying thousands of molecules of ozone.

This postage stamp from Germany depicts some of the plants and animals harmed by acid rain, a severe environmental problem in many countries.

A team of British scientists first discovered a "hole" (a very thin area) in the ozone layer over Antarctica. Satellite measurements showed that more than half the ozone there had disappeared between 1977 and 1987. Canadian scientists later discovered a smaller hole over the Arctic. Now there is evidence that ozone is thinning quickly in other parts of the world, too.

In 1990, 81 countries agreed to stop using CFCs by the year 2000 or sooner. They also set up a fund to help poorer countries reach their goal. This is one of the fastest actions to save the environment that the world community has ever taken. But it will be a long time — at least 100 years — before the ozone layer returns to what it was even in 1986.

•

The Greenhouse Effect

Carbon dioxide is the gas that makes soft drinks fizzy. It's also one of the most important gases in our atmosphere, even though it makes up less than one-tenth of one percent of it.

If you have ever sat in a car on a sunny day, you know how quickly it heats up. Rays of sunlight can come through the car windows, but the heat they cause cannot get back out. Carbon dioxide in the atmosphere acts something like that window glass. The Sun's rays pass through the atmosphere to warm our planet. Then carbon dioxide and other gases in the atmosphere trap the heat so that it cannot escape back into space. The more carbon dioxide in the atmosphere, the more heat is trapped.

In the last 150 years, the amount of carbon dioxide in the atmosphere has increased by 25 percent. Over about the same period, the world has become almost one Fahrenheit degree (about one half of one Celsius degree) warmer. The 1980s were by far the hottest decade since records have been kept. Most environmental scientists believe that human beings have caused this global warming. We have pumped enormous quantities of carbon dioxide into the atmosphere by burning fossil fuels such as coal and oil. We have also destroyed huge tracts of rainforest, releasing their stored carbon as atmospheric carbon dioxide (see p. 50).

In May 1990, 300 of the world's top experts on greenhouse gases announced their "best estimate": By the year 2020 the world will be 2.3°F (1.3°C) warmer than it is now. By 2070, it will be about 5°F (3°C) warmer. This may not seem like much, but very small changes in annual temperatures can have huge effects. A rise of about 5°F (3°C), for instance, will make Earth warmer than it has been since human beings first appeared on the planet.

Scientists cannot be sure what will happen when Earth becomes this warm, but they have made some educated guesses. Patterns of rainfall will likely change, leaving arid countries such as Somalia even drier than before. The American Midwest may see its harvest cut by about one-third as it becomes hotter and drier. New farmland will probably open up in northern Canada, but the soil there may not be good enough to make up for the lower crop yields farther south. If polar ice begins to melt, sea levels could rise by a meter or more. Low-lying areas, from Florida to Bangladesh, would be flooded, and over 200 million people all over the world could be left homeless.

Environmentalists argue that we must act now to cut carbon dioxide and other greenhouse gases. They warn that if the world waits for absolute proof that these gases cause global warming, it may be too late to avoid its catastrophic effects. As one scientist put it: "I'm not a planetary gambler."

THE GHOST PLANET

The first clear views of Mars: dust gives the sky a pink color, and iron rust makes the rocks red.

Of all the planets, Mars is the most like Earth. Its day is just a little longer than an Earth day, and it has many features that remind us of home: changing seasons, polar ice caps, and mountain ranges. For centuries, human beings hoped — or feared — there might be life on Mars. H.G. Wells imagined murderous Martian invaders in his science fiction classic, *The War of the Worlds*. In 1938, Orson Welles's dramatic radio broadcast based on this story panicked thousands of people, who believed that Martians had really landed in the United States. But other writers have created stories about peaceful beings of great intelligence who have much to teach the people of Earth.

In the late nineteenth century, several astronomers announced that they had seen straight canals crisscrossing Mars through their telescopes — evidence that we were not alone in the universe. But later observers with better telescopes could find no trace of the canals. In recent years, unmanned missions to Mars have sent back images of a waterless, lifeless planet. We've learned that a hot day on Mars is no warmer than a cold day in Antarctica. Although the atmosphere is mostly carbon dioxide — the gas that causes the "greenhouse effect" on Earth — it does not create much warmth on Mars. This is because the atmosphere of Mars is very thin, with less than one percent the pressure of our atmosphere. Yet there are signs that Mars used to be a lot more like Earth than it is now.

Billions of years ago, many active volcanoes on Mars were probably spewing out carbon dioxide and water vapor. Carbon dioxide may have formed an atmosphere 100 times thicker than the one Mars has today. Like a blanket, the carbon dioxide could hold in the Sun's heat and warm the planet. Mars may have had rainfalls and flowing water in those far-off times; it may even have had lakes and seas. But then the planet went into a deep freeze. If it ever had water, it is now locked up in ice caps or buried in permafrost, a layer of ground that never thaws.

Early Earth was probably similar to early Mars, with violently erupting volcanoes producing carbon dioxide and water. Yet Earth became a planet that could support life — and stayed that way. Scientists have several ideas about why Earth was luckier than Mars. Mars is only half as big as Earth and has only one-tenth its mass. A planet that small does not have a very strong gravitational pull. It cannot hold on to all of the gases in its atmosphere, and they gradually leak away into space.

Another difference is that on Earth everything is recycled. When rain falls, it carries some of the atmosphere's carbon dioxide down to the oceans, where the carbon becomes part of Earth's limestone. But Earth's surface is constantly shifting, buckling, and washing away. Wherever volcanoes erupt or limestone on Earth's surface is dissolved by running water, carbon dioxide is released back into the atmosphere. The surface of Mars, however, is not on the move. Any carbon dioxide washed down out of its atmosphere by long-ago Martian rainfalls became part of the ground on which it fell. The protective blanket of carbon dioxide around Mars became too thin to keep the planet warm. And Mars became a frozen desert.

But the story doesn't end there. Over the next five billion years or so, the Sun will get much hotter than it is now. Mars will warm up, perhaps enough that its ice will thaw and water will flow again. The conditions may even be right for life to evolve. The ghost planet may yet revive.

OUR ONLY HOME

A thousand years ago, half of Earth's land was covered in forests. Just over one-fifth is forested now. The tropical rainforests will be gone in less than 100 years, unless we change our ways. All over the world, other environments full of unusual plants and animals — wetlands, coral reefs, mangrove swamps — are also threatened by human beings. By the end of this century, as their natural homes disappear, about a million kinds of plants and animals will become extinct. This means that they will be lost to us forever, many without ever being named or studied.

We are finding out that when we make war on nature, we make war on ourselves. In Kuala Lumpur, for instance, people have been digging limestone out of caves and draining swamplands for farms. The caves were home to a bat called *Eonycteris spelaea*, and the swamplands were its feeding grounds. The bats began to die out, but people did not seem to care. They realized too late that the bats pollinate durian trees, which produce one of their most valuable fruit crops. With the bats almost gone, the trees cannot flourish.

The more we understand how the things in our environment are connected, the more likely it is that we can find a way to live in harmony with them. Ecology studies the way living things interact with each other, and with nonliving things such as soil, water, and air. The place where all this interaction goes on is called an *ecosystem*. A small tropical island can be an ecosystem and so can a city park, a rainforest, a woodlot, or a pond. One ecosystem provides habitats, or homes, for many different creatures. For instance, in a forest ecosystem, chipmunks burrow under gnarled tree roots, while squirrels build messy nests on swaying branches. Woodpeckers bore into the trunks to find insects that are just under the bark. Dead trees and fallen logs shelter raccoons. Even the damp, rotting leaves on the forest floor are home to busily scurrying insects.

The living things of an ecosystem also have *niches*. The niche of an arctic hare is to eat plants, provide blood for the blackflies that bite it, become food for an arctic fox, and finally return its nutrients to the soil. Think of it this way: a habitat is an address, while a niche is a job.

The relationship between the blackflies and the arctic hare is called *parasitism*. The blackflies (the parasites) benefit, but the hares, who are annoyed by their painful bites, are harmed. Sometimes living things share a relationship in which both benefit, called

Above: *In the peaceful world imagined by American artist Horace Pippin in his painting "Holy Mountain III," human beings, lions, lambs, and other creatures live in harmony on a thriving green Earth.*

Opposite page: *A small Brazilian monkey in its leafy habitat of twining rainforest vines.*

BACK TO THE GARDEN

Dr. Gilberto Ocaña checks the health of a fast-growing acacia tree in Las Pavas, Panama.

Neatly planted corn, sorghum, and cassava, growing in lines between rows of acacia trees; a small herd of goats, sheltering from the sun in an open-sided thatch-roofed shed with a slatted floor: these are scenes from a new way of life in the rural Las Pavas region of Panama. At first glance, it does not look as if anything amazing is going on here. But it is.

The usual farming method in this part of the world is slash and burn. Rainforest trees are cut down to provide poor farmland that quickly becomes exhausted. Then desperate farmers sometimes sell or rent their land for cattle grazing. Millions of rainforest acres have been destroyed this way. But Dr. Gilberto Ocaña, of the Smithsonian Tropical Research Institute, has shown that there is a better way to farm. He has introduced "alley farming" to Las Pavas.

Fast-growing acacia trees are planted in long rows. These trees have nodules on their roots that "fix" nitrogen, which means that they change it into a form that other plants can use. The crops growing between the rows of trees are enriched by the acacias without chemical fertilizers. Acacia trees in Las Pavas grow to a height of 42 feet (as tall as a four-story building) in less than four years. Some are left to grow and some are cut down for hardwood. The wood can be used for small structures (including goat shelters) and can also be sold.

Goats have not been raised in this part of the world because they cannot stand the tropical sun, but they do well if they are given shelters. In Las Pavas, the goats are fed with cassava, one of the "alley" crops. These goats provide milk, cheese, and meat — all considered gourmet treats in Panama City and other markets. Dr. Ocaña estimates that Panamanian farmers could earn twice as much per pound for the goat meat alone as they now get for beef cattle. Finally, goat manure can be collected from under the slatted floor and used for fertilizer.

If the methods used in Las Pavas become popular throughout Central America, they could not only improve the lives of rural families, but help save the rainforest as well.

symbiosis. For instance, the world's slowest-moving land animal, the two-toed sloth, has green algae growing in its fur. As the sloth hangs upside down from branches in the rainforest, it blends with its leafy home and is safe from enemies. And the algae get a warm, protected place to grow.

All the energy that fuels an ecosystem comes from the Sun. But only green plants and blue-green algae (the stuff that forms scum on ponds) can capture the Sun's energy and turn it into food. This is because they contain a chemical called chlorophyll, which gives them their green color. Chlorophyll is what chemists call a catalyst, which means that it makes things happen without getting involved in the process and without being used up. Chlorophyll lets plants use sunlight, water, and carbon dioxide to produce food in the form of sugar, and oxygen. This process is called *photosynthesis*, from the Greek words *photo*, meaning light, and *synthesis*, which means putting things together in a new way.

Other living things depend on the food made by plants (and plantlike things such as blue-green algae). Herbivores, such as sparrows, mice, rabbits, deer, horses, and cattle, feed directly on plants. Omnivores, including bears and human beings, eat both plants and meat while carnivores, such as eagles, sharks, and cougars (and your pet cat), eat mostly meat. If carnivores hunt and kill other animals, they are called *predators*. If they eat animals that are already dead,

Opposite page: This family of lions on the Serengeti Plain of Africa faces an uncertain future. Like all large carnivores, lions need big hunting territories well stocked with game. Except in protected reserves, little open land remains for these animals.

Below: This drawing shows how a rainforest forms a natural "apartment building," so that a great variety of creatures can share one habitat by living in different levels. Each of the four major layers of the rainforest is like a different world, with its own plant and animal wildlife.

they're called *scavengers*. The sight of a crow pecking at roadkill on the highway makes us shudder. But scavengers are an important part of an ecosystem's cleanup crew. Then the *decomposers* arrive to take care of what the scavengers leave behind. These fungi and bacteria break down dead plants and animals, as well as animal wastes, allowing their nutrients to return to the soil.

The living things in an ecosystem are linked together in *food chains*. In one marshland food chain, for instance, grass is munched by a grasshopper, which is then caught by a frog's sticky tongue. Next, the frog is swallowed whole by a snake, and finally, the snake is eaten by a hawk. This chain, like all food chains, starts with energy from the Sun. And it ends with a carnivore called a top carnivore because it is at the very end of the chain. Human beings are usually — but not always — at the end of a food chain. There are just a few animals that will sometimes eat people, including tigers, crocodiles, and sharks.

Most creatures eat more than one thing, and many are food for

more than one animal. For instance, a rabbit might eat several different kinds of plants, and it might be prey for an owl or a fox — or a human being. Human beings, as omnivores, eat a huge variety of things, and so they form a link in many food chains. The connections between all the different food chains in an ecosystem are called a *food web*.

Although nutrients can recycle endlessly in an ecosystem, energy cannot. This is because, at every step in the food chain, about 90 percent of the energy is lost. When a mouse eats some kernels of grain, it accumulates some of the plant's stored energy — but only a little. The mouse uses most of the energy it receives from the grain for breathing and scurrying around. So, when an owl eats the mouse, it gets much less energy than the mouse got from the grain. Because energy is lost at every stage, new energy from the Sun is always needed to keep the ecosystem humming.

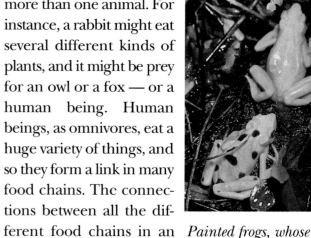

Painted frogs, whose skin can be venomous, live along riverbeds in Central Panama.

Opposite page: *Lake Natron, in the East African Rift Valley, here seen from a helicopter, has a strange red color that can be seen from space. Although it is hard to believe this could be the habitat of any living creature, the red color itself is the lake's life — teeming algae that feed on soda (the white swirls) — coming into Lake Natron from nearby volcanoes.*

Emergent layer

Canopy

Understory

Floor

BACK FROM THE BRINK

Extinction is the end of the road. It means that a particular kind of animal or plant has died out and will never be seen again. Every once in a while, a determined group of people rescue an endangered animal from this final fate. The golden lion tamarin, a squirrel-sized primate (other primates include monkeys, apes, and human beings) was almost extinct in the wild by the early 1980s. Their Brazilian rainforest home was being cut down, and they were being captured illegally as exotic pets. Only a handful survived in zoos.

A golden lion tamarin, with the magnificent reddish-gold mane that gives it its name, is learning to live in the wild again.

Now, thanks to a project started by Smithsonian scientists at the National Zoological Park in Washington, D.C., the orange-maned tamarins are being saved. A breeding program at a number of worldwide institutions built the tamarin population up to about 450. Then came the most exciting part. Ninety-five tamarins were returned to a rainforest reserve in Brazil, a few at a time. At the same time, an education program got the Brazilian people involved in protecting these rare animals. The rainforest newcomers have now produced 65 offspring in the wild, and 44 have survived. Their numbers are still very low, but it looks like the golden lion tamarin may make it back from the brink.

The most amazing comeback of any animal in recent times is one that few people know about. In 1930, a Palestinian scholar named Professor Aharoni was reading 3,000-year-old Middle Eastern texts. They often mentioned small animals, brought from Assyria, that Hittite children kept as pets. The professor was so intrigued by these "Assyrian mice" that he went to the ruins of Chaleb, an ancient Hittite city, to see if he could find any trace of them. After combing the area for a long time, the professor was thrilled to find one burrow containing thirteen tiny, light brown rodents. You have seen animals just like them many times — they were golden hamsters. Incredible as it sounds, *every* hamster in the world today is descended from the thirteen the professor discovered. Although many people have searched, no one has ever found another hamster in the wild.

Suppose a mouse needs 400 kernels of wheat to stay alive. And suppose that an owl needs five mice to feed itself. This means that it takes 2,000 kernels of grain to feed one owl. These feeding relationships form a food pyramid, with many plants at the base, some herbivores in the middle, and just one top carnivore at the apex. The owl cannot choose a less wasteful way of eating because its body cannot digest plants. But human beings usually can choose where they will eat on the food pyramid. For instance, a person who lives mainly on beef will need about ten cattle a year for food. Each of those cattle needs about an acre (half a hectare) of alfalfa to graze on. So ten acres (five hectares) of plants are needed to feed

Above: *The brilliant green color of the emerald tree boa helps to camouflage it among rainforest vines and branches.*

Opposite page: *A hilltop market in Rwanda. It is only in the last 10,000 years or so that human beings have learned how to grow their own food. But now, our numbers are outstripping our ability to feed ourselves. And our hunger for farmland is crowding out other species.*

one human being. But if that same person lives directly on plants, he or she will only need the crops grown on about half an acre of land. By "eating lower on the food chain," as it is sometimes called, human beings could make much better use of the world's resources.

As you can see from the story of the mice and the owl, top carnivores need the biggest territories to feed themselves. And now that the world is so crowded with human settlements, there are few big hunting territories left. Nearly all the world's top carnivores, including eagles, tigers, and wolves, are endangered because human beings have taken over their habitats.

Other carnivores are threatened because human carelessness has poisoned their food. Suppose a farmer spreads pesticide on a field of grain. The grain is eaten by a few mice, and the pesticide builds up in their bodies. Then all the mice are eaten by just one owl, which ends up with the biggest pesticide dose of all. In fact, many top carnivores have been harmed in just this way. A poison called DDT made peregrine falcons' eggshells so thin that nesting females crushed them. The bird was almost extinct before human beings began a rescue program.

It is tragic that we had to harm our planet so much before changing our ways. But at last, in all parts of the world, many people are concerned about saving what is left of Earth's resources. In Gibraltar, children take turns guarding nesting falcons around the clock to prevent collectors from stealing their chicks. In northern India, villagers throw their arms around trees to prevent lumberjacks from cutting them down. In your own neighborhood, perhaps, people have stopped spraying pesticides and weed-killers on their gardens because they eventually seep into rivers and lakes. Nineteen countries have signed an agreement to protect the fragile environment of Antarctica. Through the IUCN (International Union for the Conservation of Nature and Natural Resources), over 50 governments and over 300 wildlife organizations are working with scientists and local communities all over the world to mend and preserve the web of life.

A brilliantly colored Andean Cock-of-the-Rock, one of the spectacular birds endangered by the destruction of tropical rainforests. These birds eat fruit, small animals, and sometimes insects.

Above: *Human beings are just one mammal species on our Blue Planet, but we hold the fate of all the others in our hands.*

Opposite page: *The world's largest land mammals, African elephants. Their habitat is shrinking and even elephants in game reserves are threatened by poachers who kill them for the ivory in their tusks.*

THE RAINFORESTS: A DISAPPEARING TREASURE

Over 100 feet (30 meters) up, in the green canopy of the rainforest, one slip can mean a fatal fall. Yet scientists are lured up here — sometimes dangling from ropes and harnesses — because Earth's richest collection of living things can be found in these leaves and vines. Scientists used to think there were about a million different kinds of insects. But now that they are getting a look at the beetles, ants, and butterflies near the roof of the rainforest, they think the number could be more like 30 million.

The wildlife of the rainforests is incredibly rich and varied. In just one 125-acre (50-hectare) rainforest plot in Malaysia, there are over 800 different species of trees. That is about the same number found in all of North America. The Amazon River is home to 3,000 different kinds of fish, including some that eat fruit dropped by overhanging trees. Some 1,500 kinds of birds

Dr. Geoffrey Parker of the Smithsonian Environmental Research Center uses a rope and harness to reach the rainforest canopy. Emergency rescue teams and cave explorers use similar equipment.

nest in the rainforests of Indonesia. One national park in Sarawak, Malaysia, has 3,000 different kinds of butterflies, including one with a 12-inch (30-centimeter) wingspread.

Tropical rainforests once covered an area more than one and a half times the size of the United States. But almost half of this rainforest has already

been destroyed, most of it in the last 50 years. There are still about 140 million native people who hunt, fish, gather nuts and fruits, and sometimes farm in the world's rainforests, but their way of life is threatened. They are being pushed into smaller and smaller territories, where there is not enough to eat. They are catching diseases that are new to them, and many are dying. Others are moving to cities and forgetting their old way of life. The rainforest people are losing their homes. And we are losing their priceless knowledge of traditional medicines and foods.

More than one-quarter of North America's 7,000 prescription drugs come from rainforest plants, including drugs to treat malaria, heart disease, and several kinds of cancer. Corn growing wild in just one place in tropical Mexico has turned out to resist all the diseases that threaten North American corn crops. Florida citrus growers say that tiny tropical rainforest wasps are worth $30 million a year to them. These helpful creatures were brought to their state to

eat insects that attack fruit.

Unless the world changes its ways, the source of these treasures will all be gone by the middle of the next century. Every year, about 25 million acres (ten million hectares) of rainforest disappear — which is an area about the size of Pennsylvania or New Brunswick. And along with them, about 17,000 species of rainforest plants and animals are being wiped out forever. They might have been the source of drugs that could cure our deadliest diseases. But we will never know.

Why are the tropical rainforests, which are nearly all in developing countries, being cut down? Some are cleared to make way for the kinds of things that the richer countries of the world take for granted: big hydroelectric power projects; copper, gold, and iron ore mines; wide highways; and towns full of modern buildings.

In Central America, millions of rainforest acres have been cleared for beef cattle ranches. They supply some North American fast-food chains with hamburger meat — but at a

The destruction of the Amazon rainforest has caused concern all over the world. The burning of these trees is contributing to global warming, as we remove their ability to cleanse the air of carbon dioxide.

terrible cost. Cattle can only be raised on the thin, poor soil for about five years. After that, not even grass will grow.

Rainforests are also being cut down by desperately poor families who survive by "slash and burn" farming. This means that they burn off a section of trees and plant small vegetable plots. But in the rainforest, hardly any of the nutrients that make things grow are in the soil. Instead, they are stored in a thick layer of decaying plants on the forest floor. Once that is burned away, the land can support crops for only about a year. After that, the families have to burn more trees and start new garden plots. Millions of acres have been ruined this way.

At this very moment, some 75,000 fires are burning in the Brazilian rainforest. The smoke can be seen from space. But the damage may be worse than it looks. Burning the Amazon rainforest — which accounts for one-third of the world's tropical forest land — may be harming the entire planet.

Rainforests are often called "the lungs of the world." This is because the trees take carbon dioxide out of the air and replace it with oxygen and water. Without these trees to cleanse it, the air will contain more carbon dioxide. This is one of the "greenhouse gases" that are warming up the Earth's atmosphere. About half of the water that rainforest trees give off falls on them again as rain, endlessly recycling. But if the trees are destroyed, less rain falls. In the past ten years,

Panama has lost 17 inches (43 centimeters) of its annual rainfall, probably because of rainforest destruction. Many scientists think that cutting down the rainforests will change the world's climate, making it hotter and drier.

Most of the world's wealthiest countries were once covered with forest that they cleared away for farms, mines, roads, and cities. It is not really fair for those countries to lay the whole economic burden of saving the rainforests on the countries that still have them. Saving the rainforests is a task for the whole world. For instance, many environmental groups are raising money to pay for reserves of rainforest land. Governments of rich countries can refuse to give funding for projects that will damage the rainforests. Instead, they can sponsor experimental farms that use less wasteful farming techniques. And they can provide a market for renewable rainforest products. If countries can earn more by saving their tropical forests than by cutting them down, they are more likely to preserve them.

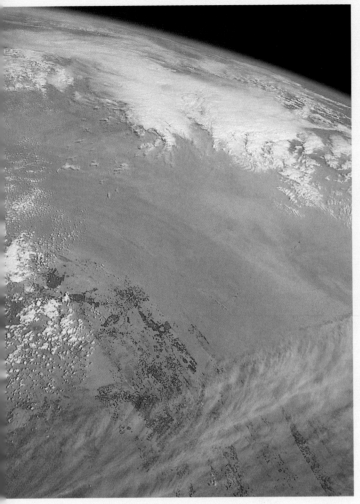

Irrigation disks (shown here as many black dots) near Riyadh, Saudi Arabia. Each of these disks is about 1 mile (1.6 kilometers) across, turned to fertile green by a pivoting irrigation system. Unfortunately, the groundwater that is pumped up for these disks is a nonrenewable resource that will soon be used up.

MYSTERIOUS DESERTS

In November 1981, the space shuttle *Columbia* turned its brand-new imaging radar system on the northeastern Sahara Desert. Carol Breed, of the United States Geological Survey, was one of the first people to look at the radar images. She was astounded by what they showed. Instead of a flat expanse of sand, there were broad valleys and a network of riverbeds. The imaging system had cut right through 15 feet (four meters) of sand and showed the buried landscape underneath. Here was proof that some of the most barren land in the world had once — about 35 million years ago — been a lush garden. At that time, the plates holding Africa and the Arabian Peninsula were welded together. Patterns of wind and rainfall were very different from the way they are now.

Today's great deserts, in North Africa and other parts of the world, were formed before human beings first appeared. Most of these deserts are in two great bands around the world, one at about 23 degrees north and the other at 23 degrees south of the equator. The winds in these regions carry little rain. Some desert lands lie in the "rain shadow" of tall mountain ranges. This means that rain-bearing clouds drop their moisture as they rise up the windward side of the mountains, leaving nothing for the parched land on the other side. Other deserts — in Asia and Australia, for instance — are in the middle of large continents, so that clouds lose all their moisture before reaching them.

Deserts have very low rainfall. They have few plants, almost no topsoil, and little water. When we think of deserts, we think of blindingly bright sand, swept by the wind into wavelike ripples and towering dunes. But only about ten percent of desert land looks like this. Deserts can be dusty, rocky or pebbly, flat or hilly. And they are not all hot. The high Gobi Desert of central Asia has below-freezing temperatures much of the year. Even Antarctica can be called a frozen desert. In all, about one-third of Earth's land is classified as arid (with ten inches/250 millimeters of rain or less a year).

Deserts expand and contract in ways that we still do not understand. In the past 200,000 years, there have been at least five "wet" periods in the Sahara. During those periods, there was enough rainfall to support people and animals on grasslands that no longer exist. Although human beings cannot control the basic processes that produce deserts, they can have a big effect on the lands at the edges of deserts. Every year, Earth is losing about 60 million acres (25 million hectares) of croplands and grasslands to *desertification* (the spreading of deserts). A billion people who now live in these lands could be driven off them by the end of this century. Millions may die of hunger. Yet human beings themselves are contributing to desertification by overusing fragile land.

In the 1960s, the region just south of the Sahara Desert, called the Sahel, was much rainier than usual. Nomadic people (people who move from place to place, herding animals) were able to move into the region with their cattle. Farming families, hungry for land in this poor part of the world, followed behind them. Then, in the 1970s, the rains stopped coming.

Streams dried up. Farmers' fields yielded fewer and fewer crops as precious topsoil turned to dust. It rose into the air in choking clouds and blew away. Hungry livestock stripped trees of their leaves, while goats dug up the roots and ate them. People became short of firewood, the only fuel most could afford. First they tried to gather only twigs, then branches, but finally they were driven to cut down the few remaining trees. Millions of the Sahel's people have died of famine in the last twenty years.

In many developing countries, people are trying to scratch a living from *marginal land,* dry land with poor soil that can easily be turned into desert. Why do they struggle to exist on such poor land? It may be because their country has so many people that no better farmland is left, or because a few wealthy landowners have taken all the good land for themselves. Poor irrigation schemes have often ruined large tracts of land by making them too salty.

Yet people can learn to preserve the land at the edge of the desert. The Baringo Fuel and Fodder Project in Kenya has saved farmland in one of the most overgrazed areas of the country. In the 1980s, local people planted fast-growing trees to anchor the soil and shelter their growing crops.

Africa's Niger River has been affected by record-breaking drought. The looming fear is that the Sahel nations of Africa may one day be as barren as Egypt's Western Desert, one of the driest regions on Earth.

Fences made of thorn bushes kept goats from eating the growing trees. The people also built low earth embankments to catch rainwater running off the fields and to stop soil erosion. The crops they are growing now are carefully chosen to suit the land and fit their needs. They plant trees, grasses, and crops that give them feed for their livestock, thatching grass for their homes, and wood for fuel, as well as providing food.

The largest reforestation project in the world is now under way in China. The massive Great Wall of China was built more than two thousand years ago to hold back Mongol invaders. Now a great "Green Wall" is going up in the same part of China, a living wall of trees to hold back the desert and keep soil from eroding. Local communities, working with government advisers, have already managed to plant a forest belt 1,000 miles (1,600 kilometers) wide and 4,000 miles (7,000 kilometers) long — almost twice the distance from New York to Los Angeles.

THE CROWDED PLANET

In a small village on the lower slopes of the Himalayas, a weary woman sets out on her daily trek to find firewood. It used to take her mother half an hour to find enough wood for the evening meal, but it takes her almost five hours. She can remember that when she was a little girl, the hillsides were thickly covered with trees, but now they are nearly bare. With no tree roots to soak up water and hold the soil, flash floods and landslides are a constant threat.

In a North American city, a man sits in a car, drumming his fingers impatiently on his steering wheel. He has a one-hour drive home to the suburbs from his office, with bumper-to-bumper traffic most of the way. Dirty yellowish air hangs heavy over the city, and fumes from the cars in front of him fill his nostrils.

Although their lives are very different, both of these people are feeling the effects of living on a more and more crowded planet.

At the time human beings were first learning to farm, about 10,000 years ago, there were less than ten million of us. The human population only reached one billion in 1800. By then, we knew enough about health care and cleanliness to lengthen our lives and allow more of our babies to survive to adulthood. In 125 more years, we doubled to two billion. And then it took just 35 years — until 1960 — to reach three billion. Fourteen more years, and we were up to four billion. In 1991, we're at five and two-fifths of a billion and we add another 95 million people every year. That's about half the population of the United States, or three times the population of Canada, in just 12 months. There are 260,000 new human beings to feed, clothe, and house every 24 hours. The United Nations predicts that there will be six billion of us before the end of this century, and ten billion jostling for space by 2025.

But the big numbers do not tell the whole story of the misery caused by our huge and growing numbers. More than 90 percent of the population increase between now and 2025 will take place in the developing countries of Africa, Asia, and Latin America. These are countries that are already having a hard time coping. According to the United Nations, almost one billion of the world's people, nearly all in developing countries, are already living in absolute poverty. This means that they have so little food that their bodies are being harmed. Many of them are starving to death.

Most of the countries that have very fast population growth also have terrible environmental problems. Land that is overgrazed turns into desert, with the last of its trees cut down for firewood. Rainforests are cleared away to provide poor farming land that will feed a family for only a year. Then, desperate people, unable to survive in this ruined landscape, move to cities looking for a better life. But most cities in developing countries can offer almost nothing to the newcomers flooding in. There are no jobs waiting for them, no school-

ing, no clean water, no housing. Many of these cities are already ringed by shanty towns where millions of people live in shacks made of sticks, cardboard, or — if they are really lucky — corrugated iron, which will at least keep out the rain. By the year 2000, 19 of the world's 25 largest cities (with 10 to 25 million people apiece) will be in the developing world.

In the rich, industrialized countries, population is leveling off and cities are not growing as fast. But many of these cities, in spite of their wealth, are unhealthy places to live. Car exhaust and factories often make the air unfit to breathe. The noise, the rush, and the crowding make people tense and sometimes violent. And although industrialized countries have less than 25 percent of the world's population, it is a greedy 25 percent that puts a great deal of strain on the planet. For instance, they gobble up about three-quarters of the world's energy supplies and steel products. They are responsible for two-thirds of the greenhouse gases going into the atmosphere (see p. 38). So while it makes sense to encourage developing countries to control their growth, it is just as important for richer countries to control their overuse of Earth's resources.

In nearly every country in the world, the birthrate — the number of babies per woman — is already going down. But many developing countries have very young populations who have not yet reached their childbearing years. This means that, even with lower birthrates, their populations will continue to grow for a time. But eventually, they will go down. In general, the more prosperous and well-educated a country's people are, the lower its birthrate. In particular, developing countries that make the effort to provide women with education and more of a voice in society are usually more successful in cutting their birthrates.

Improving the lives of people in the poorest countries may, in the long run, be the best way to keep us from overrunning the planet.

THE WORLD'S 25 LARGEST CITIES IN THE YEAR 2000
(population in millions)

World population grew, on average, by 1.7 percent each year between 1985 and 1990. At this rate it will double in 40 years. But in some developing nations, the growth rates are much higher — for instance, in Cote d'Ivoire, in Africa, the population is expected to double in just 17 years. These people are likely to suffer from crippling shortages of water, food, and land.

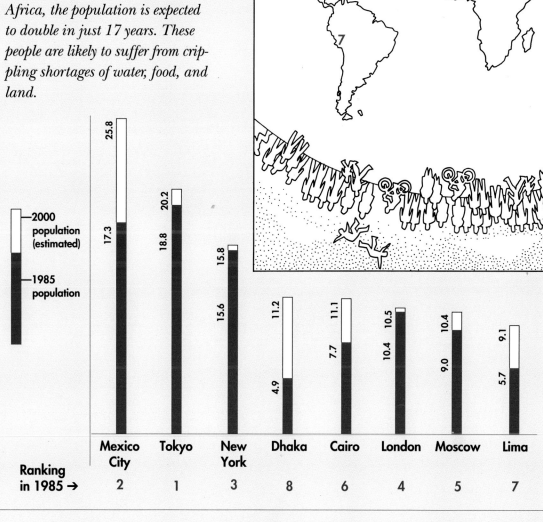

- 2000 population (estimated)
- 1985 population

City	Mexico City	Tokyo	New York	Dhaka	Cairo	London	Moscow	Lima
2000	25.8	20.2	15.8	11.2	11.1	10.5	10.4	9.1
1985	17.3	18.8	15.6	4.9	7.7	10.4	9.0	5.7
Ranking in 1985 →	2	1	3	8	6	4	5	7

55

DO WE LOVE OUR PLANET?

Earth has been around for about four and a half billion years, a length of time so great that human beings can hardly grasp it. Our earliest humanlike ancestors appeared only about two million years ago — a tiny fraction of our planet's life. For most of the time we have been here, we have walked lightly on Earth. We have only become destructive on a global scale in the last 200 years or so — when our numbers began to grow dramatically, and when we began to burn huge amounts of fossil fuels in our homes and factories. Everywhere we look today, we can see the damage we have caused — polluted air, water, and land; animal species driven to extinction; and cities and whole countries so crowded that there is little chance of a decent life for their people. It has all happened so fast, and it wasn't what we meant to do.

We thought of Earth as our domain, where we ruled over the rest of Nature and made it serve our needs. We were proud of our brainpower, proud of our medical and scientific discoveries, and proud of our inventions. In just 200 years — a tiny fraction of human existence — we have created a world of wonders: trains, cars, and airplanes; vaccines, anesthetics, and antibiotics; telephones, movies, and television; plastics; computers, satellites, and spaceships. Most of the things we have invented were intended to improve human life in some way — making it longer, healthier, and more varied. But many of them have had bad side effects we never stopped to consider. Until plastic began to overburden our waste disposal systems, for instance, it did not concern us that Earth's natural recycling systems cannot cope with these new creations. Perhaps the speed of the changes we are making, more than anything, is our undoing. We are so caught up in our idea of progress, which means bigger and bigger (buildings, industries, mines, roads, cities) and more and more (money, consumer goods) that we have spent almost no time thinking about the price we will have to pay.

Left: This postage stamp was issued in 1958 to publicize American forest conservation efforts. It appeared on the 100th anniversary of the birth of President Theodore Roosevelt, who had taken a keen interest in protecting natural resources.

Opposite page: There are still patches of serenity on our crowded planet. In Japan, a monk carefully rakes a pattern into the sand of a Zen garden.

Now Earth itself, pushed to its limits, is showing us that price in such dramatic ways that we can no longer ignore it. Earth is giving us a last chance to mend our ways — but it must be now. Fortunately, many people realize the seriousness of the situation and have already made changes in the way they live.

When you recycle paper and soda cans, or write a letter to a company complaining about its overpackaging, or spend a Saturday cleaning up a park or a creek, or make a donation to an environmental group, it may seem as if your actions are too small to matter. But taking care of Earth in these ways makes you part of a worldwide network of people, all making small changes where they live. In India, schoolchildren are made "guardians of the trees," checking on the health of trees in their area and reporting problems to the Indian Society of Naturalists. In North America, children have forced fast-food chains to use less wasteful packaging. In Kenya, the Green Belt movement, led mainly by local women, has established tree-planting programs in 60 villages, producing over two million healthy trees.

It is encouraging to know that many kinds of environmental damage can be undone if people care enough to make it happen. Here are just a few of the success stories:

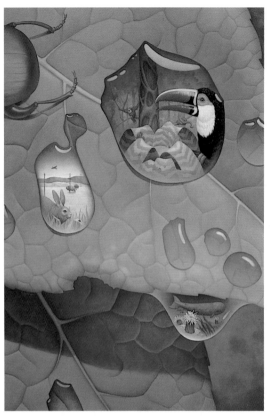

• Phosphates in detergents once threatened to kill all the fish in the lower Great Lakes. But people switched to phosphate-free detergents, and these chemicals have now almost disappeared from the lakes.

• The Arabian Oryx, a beautiful cream-colored antelope, has been saved from extinction and returned to protected lands in Oman.

• A six-year test by Norway and Canada has shown that lakes and groundwater can be returned to health if acid rain stops falling on them.

• The phasing-out of leaded gasoline in the United States cut poisonous lead emissions into the air by 60 percent between 1975 and 1986.

• Since 1973, Japan has cut by 60 percent the amount of energy and raw materials it needs to produce manufactured goods.

Another encouraging sign is the way environmental problems are being tackled by governments and international conservation organizations. Through the IUCN (International Union for the Conservation of Nature and Natural Resources), governments and wildlife organizations are working with scientists and local communities all over

Right: Robert Goldstrom's interpretation of Nature's wondrous variety shows, among other things, a tropical toucan with its huge beak and a rafflesia plant (the world's largest flower) reflected in water drops on a living green leaf.

Below: Children carrying hand-lettered placards march in Washington, D.C., on Earth Day in June 1991.

Opposite page: A boy herds cattle in Africa.

This block of U.S. postage stamps was issued in 1970 to focus attention on the problems of pollution. Clockwise, from upper left, the stamps show wheat, an urban environment, a seagull and a bluegill, as well as a view of Earth from space.

the world on projects to save the environment. In recent years, many countries have signed agreements to protect Antarctica's fragile environment, to cut sulfur dioxide emissions, and to ban ozone-harming CFCs. The United Nations' "Earth Summit," held in Rio de Janeiro in the spring of 1992, worked to produce international agreements to save the rainforests and to control "greenhouse gas" emissions.

Although some of our inventions have led us in the wrong direction, it is too simple to say that technology itself is bad. The problem is not technology, but the uses to which we put it. If our ingenuity got us into the mess we have made of our planet, it can also get us out. In the next few years, scientists all over the world will be cooperating as

never before to study our planet's problems and probe some of its mysteries. Sophisticated satellites will study the gases in Earth's atmosphere to help us understand more about global warming. International space platforms (complex satellites with many different instruments) will measure the movements of Earth's plates and try to discover more about the recycling systems of our oceans.

When the space age began, most people focused on the adventure of leaving Earth behind and exploring other worlds. And it was a great adventure. But the more we learned about other worlds, the more alien they seemed: some are frozen deserts, others are seething balls of gas. It turns out that the greatest gift space exploration has given us is a new appreciation of home. We are the first species that has ever been able to see Earth as it truly is — a unique, living Blue Planet in the blackness of space. It has helped us to change our view of Earth from something to be conquered and plundered to something to be cherished and protected. As astronaut Kathryn Sullivan put it, "I don't want to be an astronaut just because we mucked up down here and need to run away from the mess. Space exploration works as long as it's not a substitute for taking care of the Earth."

***Opposite page:** A father on an outing with his children in a Moscow park. The choices made by the countries of the world in the next few years will determine whether these children — and others all over the Earth — will inherit a healthy planet.*

CREDITS

The following abbreviations are used to identify Smithsonian Institution collections and other sources:

SI   Smithsonian Institution
HMSG   Hirshhorn Museum and Sculpture Garden
NASM   National Air and Space Museum
NMAfA   National Museum of African Art
NMAH   National Museum of American History
NMNH   National Museum of Natural History
NZP   National Zoological Park
OPPS   Office of Printing and Photographic Services
L   Left
R   Right
T   Top
B   Bottom
C   Center

Photographs from the film _Blue Planet_, distributed by Imax® Systems Corporation:

Front and back cover, title page, contents page, and pages **4, 7, 9, 12, 15, 17, 19, 21, 26, 29, 31, 33, 35, 40, 43, 45, 47, 49, 56, 59, 61**, and **62**.

Photographs from the Smithsonian Institution:

Page 5L — SI/NASM. Howard Russell Butler (1856 – 1934), _The Earth as Seen from the Moon_, before 1934, gift of H. Russell Butler, Jr.
Page 8R — SI/NMNH/Chip Clark.
Page 13 — SI/NMNH. Mural by Peter Sawyer. Photo by Chip Clark.
Page 16 — SI/NMNH/Richard S. Fiske.
Page 22 — From _Krakatau 1883_, by Tom Simkin and Richard S. Fiske (Smithsonian Institution Press, 1983).
Page 25 — SI/NMAH/Photographic Archives/ Underwood and Underwood glass stereograph collection.

Page 27R — SI/NMAH/National Philatelic Collection. Based on the Benjamin West painting, _Franklin Taking Electricity from the Sky_.
Page 27L — SI/NMAfA/Eliot Elisofon, Eliot Elisofon Archives.
Page 34 — SI/NMNH. Detail from the painting _Tower of Time_ by John Gurche. Photo by Chip Clark.
Page 38 — SI/NMAH/National Philatelic Collection. Illustration by Heinz Schillinger.
Page 41 — SI/HMSG. Horace Pippin (1888 – 1946), _Holy Mountain III_, 1945, gift of Joseph H. Hirshhorn, 1966. Photo by Lee Stalsworth.
Page 42 — SI/OPPS/Carl C. Hansen.
Page 44L — SI/Courtesy of Smithsonian News Service.
Page 44R — SI/OPPS/Carl C. Hansen.
Page 46L — SI/NZP/Dane Penland.
Page 46R — SI/NZP/Jessie Cohen.
Page 48R — SI/NZP/Jessie Cohen.
Page 50 — SI/OPPS/Richard Strauss.
Page 53 — SI/NASM/Patricia A. Jacobberger.
Page 57 — SI/NMAH/National Philatelic Collection.
Page 58L — SI/OPPS/Dane Penland.
Page 60 — SI/NMAH/National Philatelic Collection.

Photographs from the National Aeronautics and Space Administration/NASA:

Pages **5R, 20L, 36, 39**.

Additional Credits:
Page 6— U.S. Environmental Protection Agency/ S.C. Delaney.
Page 10 — Courtesy TRW Inc. Illustration by Phil Weisgerber.
Page 11 — Courtesy TRW Inc. Illustration by Henry Lozano.
Page 18 — 1987 painting by Lloyd E. Logan.
Page 23 — U.S. Geological Survey/J.D. Griggs.
Page 58T — Painting by Robert Goldstrom.

Opposite page: _A space shuttle view of the Betsiboka River Delta in Madagascar choked with silt. This terrible erosion of precious topsoil has been caused by slash and burn agriculture and overgrazing._

INDEX

ABOUT THIS BOOK

This book is based on *Blue Planet*, an IMAX® space film about Earth, which is presented by the Smithsonian Institution's National Air and Space Museum and the Lockheed Corporation in cooperation with the National Aeronautics and Space Administration (NASA). *Blue Planet* opened across North America in November 1990 and internationally in the spring of 1991. Since then it has been viewed by more than eight million people in eight countries. With stunning clarity, on screens up to eight stories high, the film presents a view of Earth that, until now, had only been seen by astronauts. Crews from five separate space shuttle missions operated the cameras that produced this living atlas of Earth.

BLUE PLANET MANIFESTED SPACE SHUTTLE MISSIONS
Most of the space footage in *Blue Planet* was filmed by the astronauts aboard the following shuttle missions:

Mission STS-61B (*Atlantis*):
November/December 1985

Commander:	Brewster H. Shaw, Jr.
Pilot:	Bryan D. O'Connor
Mission Specialist:	Mary L. Cleave
Mission Specialist:	Jerry L. Ross
Mission Specialist:	Sherwood C. Spring

Mission STS-29 (*Discovery*):
March 1989

Commander:	Michael L. Coats
Pilot:	John E. Blaha
Mission Specialist:	James F. Buchli
Mission Specialist:	Robert C. Springer
Mission Specialist:	James P. Bagian

Mission STS-34 (*Atlantis*):
October 1989

Commander:	Donald E. Williams
Pilot:	Michael J. McCulley
Mission Specialist:	Shannon W. Lucid
Mission Specialist:	Franklin R. Chang-Diaz
Mission Specialist:	Ellen S. Baker

Mission STS-32 (*Columbia*):
January 1990

Commander:	Daniel C. Brandenstein
Pilot:	James D. Wetherbee
Mission Specialist:	Bonnie J. Dunbar
Mission Specialist:	Marsha S. Ivins
Mission Specialist:	G. David Low

Mission STS-31 (*Discovery*):
April 1990

Commander:	Loren J. Schriver
Pilot:	Charles F. Bolden, Jr.
Mission Specialist:	Steven A. Hawley
Mission Specialist:	Bruce McCandless II
Mission Specialist:	Kathryn D. Sullivan

In addition, some scenes in *Blue Planet* were filmed on previous space shuttle missions:

Mission 41-C (*Challenger*): April 6–13, 1984

Mission 41-D (*Discovery*): August 30–September 5, 1984